"This small book is a gold mine of wisdom. With honest realism and beautiful vulnerability, Peter and Debbie tackle the difficult questions of marriage from a Christian perspective. I am certain that every Catholic couple will benefit immensely from reading it, discussing it, and implementing it in their marriages and families."

BISHOP SCOTT MCCAIG, CC
Military Ordinary of Canada

"This is a beautiful and timely book. Every chapter is filled with wisdom gleaned from the Master of Love, Jesus Christ, and applied to the daily struggles within marriage. I admire Peter and Debbie's honesty and humility in sharing how they battled through the various challenges they faced in their families of origin and in their own marriage and family life over the years. As a result, they are leaving a legacy of love for their children and grandchildren and offer their wisdom for how we may do the same. I would have loved to have had this book in the formative stages of my own marriage. I will recommend it enthusiastically to all the married and engaged couples I know."

BOB SCHUCHTS
Author of Be Devoted *and Founder of the John Paul II Healing Center*

"Peter and Debbie Herbeck are sharing the inside scoop on living a life with and for Jesus. This is my new handbook for implementing beautiful habits, traditions, and truths of the faith into my marriage and family culture. Peter and Debbie are courageous witnesses to the love and joy of a life lived with Jesus, and I can't thank them enough for this gift they've given the Church and the world, and most especially, to my husband, my children, and me."

JENNA GUIZAR
Founder and Creative Director of Blessed Is She

"An honest, hope-filled story of a family in love with Jesus Christ that witnesses to the drama of marriage and redeeming power of God. In these pages, you will see how Jesus Christ can make the ordinary extraordinary if we are intentional and truly desirous of Him. I recommend this to those married or discerning marriage!"

CURTIS MARTIN
*Founder and CEO of Fellowship of
Catholic University Students (FOCUS)*

"Short, easy to read, personal, and honest. This is not a theoretical tome on Catholic marriage but a real-life sharing of a real-life couple and their family that many will be inspired and helped by."

RALPH MARTIN
President of Renewal Ministries

"In *Lessons from the School of Love*, the Herbecks offer a spiritually profound and refreshingly honest guide to living marriage today. If put into practice, the wisdom found in these pages can lead any docile couple to the next level in their marriage, in their parenting, and in their relationship with God. I heartily recommend this little book!"

FR. MATHIAS THELEN
*President of Encounter Ministries and
Pastor of St. Patrick Catholic Parish*

"Peter and Debbie Herbeck are excellent examples of what they write about, and their book will be an invaluable help to married couples and to those preparing for marriage. It is Christ-centered with sound biblical and spiritual foundations. It is full of practical wisdom and years of personal experience. The reflections at the end of the chapters provide couples with the opportunity to begin implementing what they have read right away. We have known Peter and Debbie since before they were married and have seen them live out the words in this book in their marriage and family for many years. We highly recommend this book to couples. It will strengthen your marriage and deepen your relationship in the Lord."

RANDALL AND THERESE CIRNER
Authors of Ten Weeks to a Better Marriage

"I believe all married couples and couples contemplating marriage need to read this short but impactful book by Debbie and Peter Herbeck. I encourage you because of three basic reasons: (1) They are totally transparent about their own marriage. (2) It has a Scripture component. (3) They give very good recommendations on how to improve your marriage."

DANNY ABRAMOWICZ
Former NFL Player and Host of Crossing the Goal

LESSONS
from the
SCHOOL
OF LOVE

LESSONS *from the* SCHOOL OF LOVE

Cultivating a Christ-Centered Marriage

PETER & DEBRA HERBECK

Steubenville, Ohio
www.emmausroad.org

EMMAUS ROAD

Emmaus Road Publishing
1468 Parkview Circle
Steubenville, Ohio 43952

©2023 Peter and Debra Herbeck
All rights reserved. Published 2023
Printed in the United States of America

Library of Congress Control Number 2022946971
ISBN: 978-1-64585-271-1 Hardcover | 978-1-64585-272-8 Paperback | 978-1-64585-273-5 Ebook

Unless otherwise noted, Scripture quotations are taken from The Revised Standard Version Second Catholic Edition (Ignatius Edition) Copyright © 2006 by the Division of Christian Education of the National Council of the Churches of Christ in the United States of America. Used by permission. All rights reserved.

Scripture quotations marked TPT are from The Passion Translation®. Copyright © 2017, 2018, 2020 by Passion & Fire Ministries, Inc. Used by permission. All rights reserved. ThePassionTranslation.com.

Excerpts from the Catechism of the Catholic Church, second edition, copyright © 2000, Libreria Editrice Vaticana—United States Conference of Catholic Bishops, Washington, DC. Noted as "CCC" in the text.

Cover design by Allison Merrick
Layout by Emma Nagle
Photo Credit: Adobe Stock

This book is dedicated with great love and sincere thanks to our children, Sarah, Michael, Joshua, and Rachel, who have each taught us in their own unique ways what it means to love unconditionally with the heart of God.

For the ways we have failed to love you well, forgive us, learn from our mistakes, and always stay in the School of Love.

TABLE OF CONTENTS

Introduction xiii
Chapter 1: Welcome to the Battle 1
Chapter 2: Three Is Not a Crowd! 9
Chapter 3: The School of Love 17
Chapter 4: Building Our Way of Life 37
Chapter 5: Mission Possible: Helping
  Our Children Encounter Christ 47
Chapter 6: Husbands and Fathers 63
Chapter 7: Wives and Mothers 79
Chapter 8: Building a Legacy of Love 95
Chapter 9: All Things Are Possible 99
Reflection and Discussion Questions
  for Personal or Group Use 107

INTRODUCTION

> *"You learn to speak by speaking, to study by studying, to run by running, to work by working, and just so, you learn to love by loving. All those who think to learn in any other way deceive themselves."*
> —St. Francis de Sales

We have two disclaimers before you begin this book. First, as shocking as this may sound coming from its authors, *not a single word in this book will change your marriage or your family.* There is only one Word—Jesus Christ—in cooperation with your will, that has the power to change your life. We pray that as you build, and rebuild, your marriage and family life together, Jesus will be the source and center of it all.

Secondly, we do not consider ourselves experts in marriage or family. Our life together is not a storybook romance or an instruction manual. We've had marital struggles, parented very imperfectly, and haven't always invested the time and energy necessary to help grow our relationship. Sitting down to write a book together has exposed our shortcomings, but more importantly, it has also helped us ponder the goodness of God, the gift of one another, and the fruit of our love in our wonderful children and grandchildren.

Wherever you are in your own life, we humbly offer you the insights and lessons we've learned along the way. If we could invite you into our home, you would see lots of photos and hear stories that reflect an ordinary family who has earnestly yet imperfectly tried to love God and each other in extraordinary ways. An honored friend recently reminded us that marriage is a supernatural vocation, and it takes supernatural power to live it well. May God, through His merciful love and the sacramental graces of marriage, enflame your spousal love, deepen your unity, and equip you to build a legacy of love.

Debbie:

In so many ways, Peter and I couldn't be more different. I am by nature introverted, calm, and a bit shy, while Peter is an outgoing, talkative, and passionate man of action. We often laugh at the unlikely match of a Jewish girl from a wealthy Chicago suburb and a Gentile boy from a small German farming town in Minnesota. Like every married couple, we each brought our pasts with us—our families of origin with their unique qualities and traditions, as well as their dysfunctions, addictions, and well-kept secrets. It is really nothing short of a miracle that God takes our brokenness, our well-intentioned but limited human love, our past mistakes and wounds, our weaknesses and idiosyncrasies, and creates something new and beautiful. Truly, "what is impossible with man is possible with God" (Luke 18:27 NIV)! As proof that "in all things God works for the good of those who love him, who have been called according to his purpose"

(Heb 8:28 NIV), we begin this book by inviting you into the stories of our families of origin and our individual journeys toward Christ.

My journey of faith began the day I was born. As a Jew, my identity was shaped by my traditional grandparents, the Jewish community, and a religious education that culminated in my *Bat Mitzvah* (a ceremonial rite of passage) at age thirteen. My world of family, friends, and school was predominantly Jewish, and as a young child I thought everyone in the world was Jewish! By external standards, our family with four children was successful—we had a nice home, material possessions, fun vacations, and prestige within the Jewish community. But as a young child I sensed my mother's unhappiness, observed her excessive drinking, and experienced her emotional distance. My father was caring and generous, yet he wasn't able to address our family dysfunction. The clear but unspoken family protocol for handling difficult circumstances and feelings was to avoid them.

By sophomore year of high school, I had mastered the art of denial and put all my energy toward academics, athletics, and popularity. The illusion of my self-reliance was shattered one snowy December night when my older brother, a freshman in college, was killed in a car crash. I was filled with grief, anger, and confusion. My faith, expressed only through Jewish customs and traditions, now seemed shallow, if not empty. There were so many painful questions and no helpful answers. I did not know how to process my grief or make sense of this tragedy, and a powerful fear of death settled over me. Throughout the rest of high school, I studied hard to get into a good college, but on the weekends I turned to partying and promiscuity to dull my pain and find acceptance.

Introduction

Studying away from home at a large university brought new focus to my life and broadened my exposure to different kinds of people. My first roommate and other girls in my dorm not only called themselves Christians, but they claimed to know their Christian God in a personal way. I didn't know anything about Jesus and His teachings, but I had been taught that, as a Jew, Christianity was off limits.

Near the end of my freshman year, my friend Sarah invited me to watch a movie with her and her friends in the dorm lounge. If I had known it was called *Jesus of Nazareth* I never would have gone, but as I watched, I confronted the alarming and intriguing reality that Jesus was Jewish! In one scene from the movie, Jesus enters the village of Bethany and is met by a weeping woman who says, "Lord, if only you had been here, our brother would not have died." Her words, eerily similar to my own, brought back the painful memories and unanswered questions about my brother's death. I wanted to run from the room, but instead I watched as Jesus went to the tomb of His friend Lazarus, now dead for four days, and brought him back to life. I sat there stunned and wondered, who was this man who spoke life into the dead and why did people place their hope in Him?

Later that night, unable to sleep, I did the unthinkable. I borrowed my friend's Christian Bible and read the Gospels. That night I prayed to a God I wasn't even sure existed and asked, "God if you're real, show me. If Jesus is the Messiah, give me the faith to believe."

After nine months, which included that daily prayer to know the truth, examining the messianic claims of Christ, a divinely inspired dream, and a powerful vision of Christ, I was ready to welcome Jesus into my life as my Lord and Messiah. There were so many things about my life that changed for the better as Jesus became my first priority. Despite my family's disapproval and distance, I grew in faith and confidence, and the fear of death no longer gripped me. I exercised leadership gifts and helped others know Jesus. I fell in love with Peter, joined the Catholic Church, and got married. I brought my past sins into the light of the confessional. But in fear and shame, I hid the deepest wounds of my past from myself, Peter, and even God. I worked hard for God, served others, and stayed busy and focused on my responsibilities to our growing family and ministry. But there were still wounds from my past and my family of origin that affected my marriage in the areas of self-reliance, trust, and intimacy. Over the past thirty-six years I have experienced greater freedom in these areas as I've opened myself to others and to God's healing power. I have seen the beautiful fruit from living in obedience to God and His plan.

Peter:

I grew up in a small farming community in southern Minnesota, the sixth of seven children in a Catholic family. We lived one block from the cathedral parish, which included an elementary and high school. Looking back, our family life revolved in one way or another around the parish—school, sports, weekly Mass attendance, and social life all happened there. My mother was very devout, and her habit of personal prayer and a daily Rosary were the most visible expressions of faith in our home. Other than prayers at meals, we didn't pray together in any regular way as a family, nor did we have any conversations about spiritual things, at least not until years later. I don't remember my first Communion, but

Introduction

I do remember feeling nervous as I stepped behind the curtain for my first Confession. Spiritual formation, in those days, came primarily from the dedicated priests and many religious sisters who taught us in school. Looking back, the most affecting spiritual experiences, for me as a child and for our family, were centered around the celebration of Christmas and Easter, the beautiful liturgies, and our annual family rituals.

Our home life was complicated. With seven kids, there was never a dull moment. We had a full life and loving parents, but we also lived with serious dysfunction and family brokenness because of my father's battle with alcoholism. My dad's father and my dad's brother also battled alcohol addiction. Dad grew up in an alcoholic home, and he turned to alcohol as a way of coping with what today would be diagnosed as Post Traumatic Stress Disorder (PTSD). Dad was a tank commander in General Patton's Third Army in WWII, and his service included fighting in the Battle of the Bulge and the liberation of Mauthausen concentration camp.

In all my years at home, I never heard Dad speak about his experience of the war. Like many soldiers of his time, he returned from the war rightly recognized as a hero, but at the same time, acutely aware of the terrors of war. He simply wanted to leave it in the past. Drinking seemed the only thing that he and some of his buddies could do to numb the pain, memories, nightmares, and guilt. He went through alcohol treatment a few times in my early childhood, but often after a few months, he would be back at it. He couldn't seem to live without it. His drinking patterns were irregular—once a week to once every two weeks. When he was sober, which was most of the time, he was a good father, and an active leader in the parish and in the political life of the community. When he drank, it was a different story. He would never physically hurt anyone, but all the pain and anger, mostly directed at himself, would come out. Until my junior year of high school, our family lived on a roller coaster of fear, confusion, pain, anger, and shame, which we rarely talked about. There are many painful memories from those years, but thanks be to God, that's not the end of the story! In God's great mercy, He chose to reveal Himself to us in the place of our greatest pain and source of shame.

During my junior year of high school, my oldest sister Kathy, who was married, came home to share something very important with our family. That Saturday night when my father was out drinking, we gathered at the kitchen table, and what transpired opened a new world to me. Kathy seemed different. She was passionate and alive with faith. She told us that she belonged to a prayer group in her parish. It was the first time I had heard someone in my family speak the name of Jesus with such familiarity and conviction. Kathy revealed that her weekly prayer group had been praying for Dad for the past six months. Recently, one of the men had told her that God had heard our cry, that He was going to heal our dad, and that it was important for our family to come together and entrust our lives to Him. That moment was a paradigm shift. I remember thinking, "A farmer in northern Minnesota heard God say something about our family? Is this true?" We had often approached my father's addiction as a cross we were all meant to bear. Kathy reminded us that Jesus was alive and that He had a different plan. If we wanted to see Dad healed, it was crucial we believe this. Her words penetrated my heart, and later that night I got down on my knees and for the first time since elementary school, I asked Jesus to

Introduction

help me believe and to bring healing to Dad. There was nothing more I wanted than to see my father healed.

A few weeks later, I was doing homework and waiting for my dad to come home. He came in late and sat down next to me. I smelled the booze on his breath. After a few moments he said my name, he reached down and grabbed my arm, and with a tear in his eye said, "Son, I'm a sick man, and I need help." That was the first time I heard him admit that he had a problem. A few days later he checked himself into a rehab center for four weeks of inpatient treatment. We joined him as a family once a week. It was the most challenging, healing, and transformational experience we ever shared as a family. At the end of those long, difficult weeks, Dad stood up in front of a roomful of people and said, "My name is Joe Herbeck, I am an alcoholic; I cannot live without God in my life." Dad lived the next twenty years sober. They were the last and, arguably, best years of his life. Just a few years after Dad's healing, all seven Herbeck kids either renewed or returned to the faith in a life-changing way. Jesus became the center of our individual lives and our family.

We grew closer as a family and came into deeper emotional and spiritual health. We acquired tools that helped us face the pain, dysfunction, and shame that so often accompanies addiction. My father's funeral in the neighborhood cathedral church was filled with family and friends who had seen the transformation in Dad and in our whole family. In his eulogy, I shared that it was in our weakness that God's strength was manifest in us. God provided the grace my father needed to humble himself and to admit he was powerless over the alcoholism that had gripped his life. The Lord's goodness and our process of family healing became an important foundation and a source of confidence, hope, and strength for my own marriage.

Marriage doesn't automatically heal past wounds and make everything better. It takes intentional and consistent effort and a desire for deeper personal healing to allow this beautiful and holy vocation to grow and serve its intended purpose. God in His merciful love is offering to help to teach us, both as individuals and as a couple, how to truly love each other and our family.

Chapter 1

WELCOME TO THE BATTLE

Thirty-six years ago, united in the Sacrament of Matrimony, we began an exciting and mysterious adventure. We charted a course for our lives that wasn't based merely on romantic feelings or wishful thinking. Although we had some financial, family, and career goals, one principal aim informed the rest. Our deepest desire was to live with God forever and to help one another, our future family, and those God placed in our lives to know Jesus and get to heaven. This lofty objective seemed abstract to us as we planned our wedding, but as we settled into married life and our family grew, we quickly saw the need for a concrete, practical plan to help us be a family destined for heaven.

Today, God's plan for marriage and family is at the center of an intense spiritual battle. In our current culture, and to some degree within the Church today, the language of "spiritual battle" is considered extreme, negative, outdated, or even psychologically and spiritually unhealthy. Of course, the opposite is true. To understand that our lives are engaged each day in spiritual combat is to see things as they really are, as our Lord sees them.

An important first step in building a strong marriage and family culture is to perceive the spiritual context in which we live and to understand the forces that are set against us.

In 1 John 5:19 we are reminded that "The whole world lies under the power of the evil one." The *Catechism of the Catholic Church* summarizes our situation:

> This dramatic situation of "the whole world [which] is in the power of the evil one" makes man's life a battle: The whole of man's history has been the story of dour combat with the powers of evil, stretching, so our Lord tells us, from the very dawn of history until the last day. Finding himself in the midst of the battlefield man has to struggle to do what is right, and it is at great cost to himself, and aided by God's grace, that he succeeds in achieving his own inner integrity. (CCC 409)

Everyone who seeks to follow Jesus and help their children do the same must come to terms with these inescapable facts. (1) We live in the midst of a battle. (2) We are engaged in "dour combat with the powers of evil." (3) It requires daily struggle. (4) The cost of this struggle will be great. (5) God promises to give us all the grace we need to win this battle.

The struggle is inescapable because we live in enemy-occupied territory. The Church is a resistance movement against the powers of this world. The fundamental forces we must resist every day are threefold: the world, the flesh, and the devil. The "world," in the biblical sense, is the fallen dimension of God's good creation—the political, social, cultural, economic, and volitional forces that resist the will of God. One example is the continued aggressive expansion, promotion, and celebration of abortion throughout the world right up to, and in some cases beyond, the child's first breath through political and legal means, fully supported by propaganda through media and the entertainment industry. Today's "cancel culture" provides a vivid example of the world's attempt to intimidate Christians into accepting the redefinition of family, human sexuality, and human identity itself.

The "flesh" is the enemy within. It is the tendency toward sin, the inclination to not trust God and to seek one's own will rather than God's. The flesh includes our minds, which are also subject to disordered impulses such as pride, envy, or greed.[1] The flesh is like a Trojan Horse, weakening us from within. The *Catechism* identifies its origins:

> As a result of original sin, human nature is weakened in its powers, subject to ignorance, suffering and the domination of death, and inclined to sin (this inclination is called concupiscence). (CCC 418)

Each of us has a personal story of our struggle against sin. We come into marriage as imperfect people, weak and broken, each with our own interior struggles with temptation, habitual patterns of sin, and a history of successes and failures in our battle against the flesh. The flesh is often the primary battleground through which the devil will seek to prevent us from the challenging task of building a family culture.

---

[1] See Galatians 5:19–21 for St. Paul's list of the works of the flesh.

The pressure from the powers of this world to conform to its ways is directed toward the flesh. The fear of others' opinions, rejection, public embarrassment, losing financial security, comfort, or standing in society, and inordinate self-love weaken resolve. If these temptations of the flesh are not subdued by a deeper trust and surrender to the Holy Spirit, we will find the idea of authentic marital love and building a countercultural family life too difficult. St. Paul speaks directly to this deep struggle in the human heart:

> For those who live according to the flesh set their minds on the things of the flesh, but those who live according to the Spirit set their minds on the things of the Spirit. To set the mind on the flesh is death, but to set the mind on the Spirit is life and peace. For the mind that is set on the flesh is hostile to God; it does not submit to God's law, indeed it cannot; and those who are in the flesh cannot please God. . . . for if you live according to the flesh you will die, but if by the Spirit you put to death the deeds of the body you will live. (Rom 8:5–8, 13)

And finally, our great enemy is the devil, Satan, who Jesus calls a murderer and a liar (see John 8:44). He manipulates the world and constantly tempts our flesh to connive with him against God. The Apostles make it clear that our battle is not against human beings; instead we are up against real spiritual forces—fallen angels, who hate God:

> Finally, be strong in the Lord and in the strength of his might. Put on the whole armor of God,

that you may be able to stand against the wiles of the devil. For we are not contending against flesh and blood, but against the principalities, against the powers, against the world rulers of this present darkness, against spiritual hosts of wickedness in the heavenly places. (Eph 6:10–12)

St. Peter reminds us that this daily battle demands vigilance and action on our part: "Be sober, be watchful. Your adversary the devil prowls around like a roaring lion seeking some one to devour. Resist him, firm in your faith, knowing that the same experience of suffering is required of your brotherhood throughout the world" (1 Pet 5:8–9).

Despite the sobering reality of what we are up against, the Lord wants us to know that He is with us every step of the way. Like every disciple and every couple seeking to seriously follow the Lord, Debbie and I have faced times of real discouragement, fear of the future, anxiety about our kids, and conflicts in our marriage. But looking back we can say with certainty that the promises of God are true!

"I will never fail you nor forsake you." (Heb 13:5)

"My grace is sufficient for you, for my power is made perfect in weakness." (2 Cor 12:9)

"I can do all things in him who strengthens me." (Phil 4:13)

"Seek first his kingdom and his righteousness, and all things shall be yours as well." (Matt 6:33)

> *"For all who are led by the Spirit of God are sons of God. For you did not receive the spirit of slavery to fall back into fear, but you have received the spirit of sonship. When we cry, 'Abba! Father!' it is the Spirit himself bearing witness with our spirit that we are children of God." (Rom 8:14–16)*

The Battle for the Family

As we reflected on our family life, the biblical worldview was a key element to forming a family culture centered on Christ. A culture is a pattern of life built on a common worldview. For centuries, the broader culture, especially in Europe and North America, was informed by a Judeo-Christian worldview. In fact, it was referred to as a Christian culture, or Christendom. As a result, there was almost universal support for a biblical view of marriage, family, human sexuality, and sexual identity as being male and female. That broader public support, which privileged the traditional view of marriage, reinforced the efforts of parents seeking to raise their children in the Lord. That has all changed. We are in an entirely new situation. The moral and imaginative vision of the worldview that informed the broader culture is gone. We are living through epic change, which includes a radical rejection of the Judeo-Christian understanding of the human person, marriage, family, sexual identity, and gender. For the first time in American history, the biblically informed national consensus on marriage and family that existed since the founding of our country has become the countercultural position.

Underlying this change is an ever-intensifying spiritual battle that has taken a particular turn in our time. The Judeo-Christian family has become ground zero of a ferocious spiritual battle. Pope Emeritus Benedict XVI described the battle:

> But the real threat to the Church and thus to the ministry of St. Peter consists . . . in the worldwide dictatorship of seemingly humanistic ideologies, and to contradict them constitutes exclusion from the basic social consensus.[2]
>
> A hundred years ago, everyone would have thought it absurd to speak of homosexual marriage. Today whoever opposes it is socially excommunicated. The same applies to abortion and the production of human beings in the laboratory.[3]
>
> Modern society is in the process of formulating an 'anti-Christian creed,' and resisting it is punishable by social excommunication. The fear of this spiritual power of the Antichrist is therefore only too natural, and it truly takes the prayers of a whole diocese and the universal Church to resist it.[4]

These "humanistic ideologies" are fueled by the "spiritual power of the Antichrist" and have led to the formulation of a new "anti-Christian creed." In a letter written by Sr. Lúcia of Fatima to Cardinal Carlo Caffarra, she communicated the Blessed Mother's message to her:

> The final battle between the Lord and the reign of Satan will be about marriage and the family.

---

[2] Peter Seewald, *Benedict XVI: A Life*, vol. 1, *Youth in Nazi Germany to the Second Vatican Council 1927–1965* (London: Bloomsbury), 534.

[3] Seewald, *Benedict XVI: A Life*, 1:534.

[4] Seewald, *Benedict XVI: A Life*, 1:534–535.

> Don't be afraid, because anyone who operates for the sanctity of marriage and the family will always be contended and opposed in every way, because this is the decisive issue . . . however, Our Lady has already crushed its head.[5]

Although we are in the midst of a battle and the world around us often looks bleak, we can draw strength and courage from knowing that the victory has already been won, and the one who is in us is greater than the one who is in the world (1 John 4:4).

---

[5] Voce di Padre Pio Radio, Interview with Cardinal Caffara, trans. Francesca Romana, reproduced for Rorate Caeli, "Cardinal: "What Sister Lúcia told me: Final Confrontation between the Lord and Satan will be over Family and Marriage," https://rorate-caeli.blogspot.com/2015/06/cardinal-what-sister-lucia-told-me.html?m=1.

Chapter 2

THREE IS NOT A CROWD!

Like many people, Peter and I naively believed that marriage would solve the problems we brought with us and those that would come. Our very different family backgrounds, life experiences, temperaments, and the adjustment of blending our lives created unforeseen challenges and at times agitated our personal wounds and weaknesses. Despite all of this, we had *the most important thing* going for us. Years before we met, God was at work in each of our lives. In the exact same year, many miles apart, we both had a powerful encounter with the Person of Jesus, accepted His invitation to live as His disciples, and to seek first the kingdom of God.

I, Peter, remember a time when I understood the call to discipleship in a deeper way. I was twenty, living in my college dorm, and just beginning to develop the habit of reading Scripture daily. One morning, I was reading the sixth chapter of Matthew, in which Jesus exhorts His disciples to "not be anxious about tomorrow." Instead of worrying, Jesus gives the following command and a promise: "But seek first his kingdom and righteousness, and all these things will be yours as well" (Matt 6:33).

At that moment, for the first time in my life, a Bible passage seemed to jump off the page and pierce my heart. It became a living word spoken directly to me. I sensed Jesus saying to me: "If you make this command your life's mission and purpose, I will show you my faithfulness, I will fulfill this promise." Early on, God was underlining the fundamental approach He wanted me to have in my life. And so, I began to try in practical, not just abstract theoretical, ways to put Him first in all things.

As we both grew in our faith, our lives were far from perfect, but we cultivated habits of daily personal prayer, Scripture study, and reception of the sacraments. Living in Christian community with accountability and formation also helped root us in Christ. In short, we each placed Jesus at the center of our lives. Tim Keller describes so clearly the sobering reality of surrender and living under the Lordship of Jesus:

> What it means to live a Christian life is that you put to death the right to live life as you choose. You put to death the idea that you belong to yourself. You put to death the idea that you know best what should happen in your life. You put that to death, and you give it to God.[1]

Our engagement period was exciting but stressful as we planned our Catholic-Jewish wedding amidst family expectations and sensitivities. The day finally arrived, and we stood beneath the traditional Jewish wedding canopy (Chuppah), before our priest and a rabbi, surrounded by Debbie's Jewish family, friends, and our brothers and

---

[1] Timothy Keller, "Everyone with a Gift," video, September 18, 2011, uploaded August 10, 2015, https://www.youtube.com/watch?v=KmpwVmssS_Q.

sisters in Christ. It was a beautiful and joyful day, yet also a clear reminder of how much we needed the grace and power of God to deepen our love and unity and overflow into the lives of those we loved. In that first year as we learned to live together and we welcomed our first child, we daily faced big and small opportunities to put aside our preferences and set each other's needs before our own. As our family grew, the demands of life and little ones taught us how to sacrifice our time, sleep, leisure, and money toward a greater good.

Give God Permission

Just as we had done in our individual lives, together we actively and intentionally put our marriage under the Lordship of Jesus and began with the right foundation. We didn't just invite the living God into our well-intentioned plans, we gave Him permission to show us His plan for our life together, and as He did, we stepped into it. It was a huge relief to know that God was in control and that we could trust Him in all things. At times when finances were tight, parenting was difficult, or family members didn't agree with our decisions, we were tempted to take back the reins and rely on our own limited strength and resources. On those occasions, we reminded one another that *unless the Lord builds the house, its laborers* (no matter how hard we work!), *labor in vain* (Ps 127:1). Anyone who has been married more than five years can tell you that physical and sexual attraction, compatibility, and common interests (which are all parts of the house, but not the foundation) are not enough to sustain and deepen a marriage. *When*, not *if* the storms of life come, and we are pushed beyond our human strength and understanding, we will discover whether the foundation of our marriage has been built upon the rock or shifting sands.

We implemented some very practical ways to keep God at the center and to express our trust in Him. We made sure that personal prayer and the sacraments were an integral part of each day and week. As our family grew and my life with small children was quite consuming, Peter made sure I had time for uninterrupted personal prayer and Scripture study. We encouraged one another to seek out support from the broader Catholic community through men's and women's groups and mentorship from older married people. Our continued growth as disciples, as a married couple, and as parents showed us how necessary were the other people in our lives (usually older and wiser), who could offer guidance and prayer. This required humility, and it was never easy to disclose mistakes, marital conflict, or a struggling child, but when we chose to submit ourselves to the help and wise counsel of others, God always provided what we needed. We were shaping our marriage and family together as a couple, but we didn't want to just make it up as we went along. So, we relied on the wisdom of Scripture and the teaching of the Catholic Church, even when it was difficult or contrary to those around us. We chose to not use contraception and instead practiced Natural Family Planning. We prayerfully considered how many children to have and when to have them, and always remained open to new life. We chose to honor the Lord's Day every Sunday. Mass was non-negotiable, regardless of other important activities (even sports!), and we took intentional time together as a family to rest and relax. Practical expressions of the decision to put Christ first unfolded as our family grew (see Chapter Four), and we often needed to renew our commitment to give everything to God.

We had an opportunity to entrust our lives and our future more deeply to the Lord when our kids began attending Catholic school. We stood at a crossroads; should I (Peter) continue working full-time in Catholic ministry (which wasn't very lucrative), or pursue a secular job that provided more money for our growing family? As I prayed, I sensed the Lord's love and blessing in either choice. But God made it clear to me that what was driving me was fear and a lack of trust in His provision. As Debbie and I took time together and separately to pray more about this, the Lord began to reveal to us His faithfulness and provision in concrete ways. Within a few weeks, we received significant sums of money from three separate people—money we didn't ask for. One night shortly after receiving these gifts and the answer to our prayers, we went downstairs to a small room designated for prayer. We knelt together and placed before the Lord our wallets, house and car keys, a family photo—things that were symbolic of our life together. We prayed, "Lord, we trust you. Once again, we put our whole life under your Lordship and we give you permission to lead and guide us. Everything we have belongs to you, we are just stewards of what you've given us." Our four children all received Catholic school and college educations, and we are still working full-time in ministry. God has abundantly provided for all our needs as we have sought first His kingdom.

We believe that every family should have their own motto that articulates their identity and motivates their decisions. Ours is taken from St. Paul's words in 2 Corinthians 5:9: "We make it our aim to please the Lord." This sounds like a noble yet abstract ideal, yet we quickly discovered that making it our aim to please the Lord had some very practical implications in our marriage and family.

One of the memorable examples that set the tone for our married life came shortly after our honeymoon. I came home one evening and Debbie was upset with me about something, but I couldn't figure out what was going on. Back then, we didn't know how to communicate very well when we were angry or upset with each other. Her tendency was to get quiet and my approach was, "If you have something to say, just say it!" I was an insecure, newly married guy and in my frustration, I blew up and yelled at Debbie. Then I went for a walk, and when I returned she was asleep. I went to bed thinking self-righteously, "Hey it's her fault, not mine." I had an inkling that I should try to do something to repair the damage, but I held fast to my desire to be right. The next morning, I got up early to pray, and I sensed the Lord telling me, "Peter, you can't talk to Debbie just any way you want. She is my daughter. It's okay to get angry, but don't shout and call names because it is hurtful." I sensed the Lord instructing me to go upstairs and ask Debbie to forgive me. My first response was, "No way, it's not my fault." But I felt the gentle, loving presence of the Holy Spirit pressing in on me and reminding me of the Scripture passage that says, "Be angry but do not sin" (Eph 4:26). I asked Deb to forgive me, which she did. We both repented for treating each other in ways that were not loving and did not please God. We took out index cards and wrote down our "do's" and "don'ts" based on Scripture for handling the conflicts that would inevitably come. We agreed to learn how to express our anger in healthier ways by not screaming, calling names, or shutting the other out, to quickly repair our rifts and offenses through forgiveness, to not "let the sun go down on our anger" and to honor and respect one another, particularly in the area of speech (Eph 4:26). That important lesson early on became the foundation for not only how we related to each other, but for modeling to and teaching our children. Our aim wasn't just to please ourselves, or even one another, but to please the Lord.

Chapter 3

THE SCHOOL OF LOVE

When our oldest daughter got married, the priest who celebrated the Mass was a close family friend. I, Debbie, remember Father's homily that day, directed not only to the newly married couple, but to each of us. He observed that many couples choose the reading from I Corinthians 13:

> Love is patient, love is kind. It does not envy, it does not boast, it is not proud. It does not dishonor others, it is not self-seeking, it is not easily angered, it keeps no record of wrongs. Love does not delight in evil but rejoices with the truth. It always protects, always trusts, always hopes, always perseveres. Love never fails. (I Cor 13:4–8 NIV)

Father then looked at the happy, wide-eyed couple, smiled, and said, "Love never fails. Isn't that nice? Isn't that beautiful? Actually, love fails all the time!" His words weren't sugar-coated, idealized notions of marriage. He didn't talk about how much fun they would have together, but instead, on one of the most important days of their lives, Sarah and Rick heard a sobering reality: human love often fails, even within the Church. The good news is that with Christ at the center of a marriage, all things are possible! Christian marriage is the school of love, where despite the limits of our own love, we can discover Christ's presence and power to teach us to love one another with the Love that never fails.

The *Catechism* tells us that "Love is the fundamental and innate vocation of every human being" (CCC 2392). Reflecting on this challenging call to love, at times I've selfishly pondered why my fundamental vocation couldn't be cooking, gardening, playing tennis, reading, or watching college basketball. These are the things I'm good at or enjoy doing! Our vocation isn't fundamentally about *what* we do, it's about *who* we are and what we are made for. We are created in the image and likeness of God, who is love, and in a beautiful and profound way, the mutual love of a man and woman becomes an image of the absolute and unfailing love of God for mankind (see CCC 1604).

The whole point of our lives is to love and be loved, to become like *God who is love*. For those of us who are called to marriage, this means our vocation is the place—the school—where we daily learn to love in ways we never would if we lived alone. In this school of love, it's not just Peter and I working hard to figure it out. There is a third Person, an instructor, God Himself, who is present not just on the first day of school (our wedding) or remotely like an online class, but every day He is within us, teaching and empowering us to be better lovers. Reverend Fulton Sheen described this so well:

It takes three to make love. What binds lover and beloved together on earth is an ideal outside both. As it is impossible to have rain without the clouds, so it is impossible to understand love without God.[1]

Do I Really Know How to Love?

One Saturday morning, about ten years and four kids into our marriage, amid family chores, uncooperative little helpers, and my own grumbling, I had this disturbing realization that I still didn't know how to love very well, especially those closest to me. God clearly didn't want my epiphany moment to dishearten me but rather to motivate me to grow in a more mature love. My ideas about love were still somewhat influenced by a more contemporary, worldly understanding. Simply stated, St. Thomas Aquinas' definition of love is "willing the good of the other" (CCC 1766). Fr. Thomas Dubay fleshes out this notion:

> The gospel definition of love goes something like this: a self-sacrificing, willed concern for and giving to another, even if attraction and feeling are diminished or absent, and even if little or nothing is received in return—and all with divine motivation.[2]

It can be easy when dating to put your best foot forward—to experience "being in love" when the

---

[1] Fulton J. Sheen, *Three to Get Married* (New Jersey: Scepter Publishers, 1951), 51.
[2] Thomas Dubay, S.M., *Deep Conversion, Deep Prayer* (San Francisco: Ignatius Press, 2006), 68.

excitement and romantic feelings are at their high point. C. S. Lewis expresses this reality and the need to move to a deeper more abiding love:

> Love in this second sense—love as distinct from "being in love"—is not merely a feeling. It is a deep unity, maintained by the will and deliberately strengthened by habit; reinforced by (in Christian marriages) the grace which both partners ask, and receive, from God. They can have this love for each other even at those moments when they do not like each other; as you love yourself even when you do not like yourself . . . "Being in love" first moved them to promise fidelity: this quieter love enables them to keep the promise. It is on this love that the engine of marriage is run: being in love was the explosion that started it.[3]

Many of us enter marriage and family life with an idealized view of what it will be like. I could not fully understand that I would need to learn a whole new way of loving that had very little to do with my feelings, and I would be tested and refined through the call to daily lay down my life for others.

> The promise, made when I am in love and because I am in love, to be true to the beloved as long as I live, commits me to being true even if I cease to be in love. A promise must be about things that I can do, about actions: no one can promise to go on feeling a certain way. He might as well

---

[3] C. S. Lewis, *Mere Christianity* (New York: Touchstone, 1996), 100.

promise to never have a headache or always to feel hungry.[4]

We can also come into marriage with fears and low expectations based on our own experiences and observations of our parents' failed or unhealthy relationships. Jesus desires to deliver us from self-protection and fear of failure and to give us the grace and tools we need to build a marriage of deep love and fidelity.

No Greater Love

When asked what was the greatest commandment, Jesus replied: "You shall love the Lord your God with all your heart, and with all your soul, and with all your mind. This is the great and first commandment. And a second is like it, You shall love your neighbor as yourself" (Matt 22:37–39). Jesus defined love of God as the first and greatest thing a human being can do. There is literally nothing of higher value than to love God in this total way. What flows then from this first love is love of neighbor. Jesus, in speaking to St. Catherine of Siena, articulates the reason He calls us to love our neighbor.

> I ask you to love me, with the same love with which I love you. But for me you cannot do this, for I love you without being loved. Whatever love you have for me you owe me, so you love me not gratuitously but out of duty, while I love you not out of duty but gratuitously. So you cannot give me the kind of love I ask of you. This is why I have put you among your neighbors: so

[4] Lewis, *Mere Christianity*, 107.

that you can do for them what you cannot do for me—that is, love them without any concern for thanks and without looking for any profit for yourself. And whatever you do for them I will consider done for me.[5]

What does it mean to love God with all of one's heart, soul, and mind, and how is it to be expressed? St. John the Evangelist tells us, "We know love by this, that he laid down his life for us; and we ought to lay down our lives for the brethren" (1 John 3:16). Jesus demonstrated what love looks like; He defined its essence by laying down His life. Jesus' death on the Cross, an offering for our sins, was the supreme act of love that brought salvation to the world (1 John 2:1–2, 2 Cor 5:21). In laying down His life Jesus not only took away sin but also taught us how we are meant to live and love. He showed us that love, at its deepest level, is sacrificial. It comes at great personal cost, and its sacrificial quality is what makes it distinctively Christian. As followers of Jesus, we are called to "follow God's example . . . and walk in the way of love, just as Christ loved us and gave himself up as a fragrant offering and sacrifice to God" (Eph 5:1–2 NIV). In marriage, husbands are called to love their wives, as Christ loved the Church and gave Himself up for her (Eph 5:25). Kingdom love is an exchange; it is an emptying of oneself for the good of another. Christ is the supreme model for us: He empties Himself in the Incarnation, and He dies to Himself in the Crucifixion, so that we might be raised to new life with Him in the Resurrection.

---

[5] St. Catherine of Siena, *The Dialogue* (New Jersey: Paulist Press, 1980), 121.

Christian family life is rooted in the self-donating love between a father and a mother who are seeking to imitate Jesus' love. Therefore, the cost of married love is significant, and the sacrifices required will entail suffering. The most immediate sacrifice will likely be the experience of having to put someone else first. This means an exchange—something in me must die in order to allow something (or someone) else to live and grow. The self typically dies a slow, painful death. That is why Jesus made "denial of self" the first condition of becoming one of His disciples: "If any man would come after me, let him deny himself and take up his cross and follow me" (Matt 16:24). To deny oneself is to say no to the constant temptation and habit of the flesh to say, "My will be done." Christian marriage and family life is a community of disciples formed by Jesus, through the power of the Holy Spirit, who are learning together how to say to the Lord, "Thy will be done." Christian family life is not simply the result of human effort; it is a miracle, a work of grace. It will take all of our effort, but the sacrificial love that the Lord is leading us into through marriage and family is far beyond our natural strength alone. It is His work in and through us.

This is why every family needs to be engaged in the sacramental life of the Church. We need the graces and the power the Lord gives us through them. Above all, the Holy Eucharist must be at the center of family life. I marvel at God's great wisdom in giving us this Sacrament. Jesus' once and for all perfect sacrifice is represented to us at every Mass. His plan is to gather all of His family every Sunday throughout the world to teach us, to feed us, and to strengthen us. We come together, young and old, to bow down before this great mystery, and by a miracle of the Holy Spirit, Jesus' supreme act of saving love is made present. And we remember what matters most. We hear, see, and touch what gives us our identity, purpose, and destiny. In the Holy Sacrifice of the Mass, we are reminded that Jesus fulfilled the two great commandments to perfection. First, "being found in human form, he humbled himself and became obedient unto death, even death on a cross" (Phil 2:8) and second, "Greater love has no man than this, that a man lay down his life for his friends" (John 15:13). Because of His suffering and death, we don't have to be afraid of the sacrifices and sufferings that marriage and family will necessarily entail.

Every marriage has its trials. Some families carry heavy burdens with great suffering, through the death of a child or spouse, severe sickness or physical handicaps, miscarriages, infertility, financial crises, mental illness, or addictions of various kinds. We've had the privilege of knowing some extraordinary families who have walked through these kinds of trials with heroic faith, hope, and love.

Often the smaller daily challenges of life can become sources of trial—even suffering. The sheer weight of busy schedules, never-ending meals and messes, tuition bills, carpools, and more can cause significant stress. So much of family life is characterized by the small, hidden acts of love. Sometimes we can wonder if our efforts make any difference.

Jesus wants us to know, without a doubt, that He notices and remembers every act of love, no matter how small. He said He will remember and reward the one who gives a cold cup of water to another who was in need of it (Matt 10:42). When we know that the small acts of sacrificial love that characterize most of our days as spouses and parents are seen and valued by the Lord, it gives significant meaning to our lives and an ability to persevere in love even when it is difficult.

Lessons from the School of Love

One of the many qualities I, Debbie, admire in Peter is his love of learning. Our family room is lined with shelves filled to overflowing with books (mostly spiritual) that Peter has collected over the years. Nowadays, he also turns to podcasts, audiobooks, and YouTube videos to satiate his hunger for knowledge. Even if we are past school age, each of us are perpetual learners in the school of love. Whether we are eager or less enthusiastic, there are valuable lessons to be learned and relearned that are intended to make us more like Jesus.

Lesson #1: Love Is Generous

During our short engagement, Peter took me back to Minnesota to meet the family he had lived with during college. We were having a nice conversation in the living room when Peter excused himself to use the bathroom. Almost on cue, the husband and wife leaned in closer to me, eager to relate some top-secret information about my future spouse. "We know Peter very well," they began, "and we think it's really important for you to be prepared to share him with many others throughout the course of your married life." I responded in a low-key way, "For sure, I'm not the possessive type!" They countered, "God is going to call you in ways that you don't understand right now, and you need to be ready to share him with the whole world."

I honestly thought they were just reaffirming what I already knew—that Peter's big and passionate personality would draw many people into our life. But I tucked away their wisdom and as our life together unfolded, I began to understand and see that God had a plan for us as a married couple and particularly for Peter's life. As his wife, I was drawn in, not as an accessory but as one half of the whole. Even if I never went with Peter to his speaking engagements, his mission was our mission now. That conversation also helped me begin to grasp a reality that wasn't always so apparent during the engagement and wedding preparations. We were embarking on a challenging adventure that wasn't essentially about the two of us accumulating stuff, having kids, decorating a house, planning vacations, and pursuing careers. It wasn't about getting, it was about giving; it wasn't about settling in, it was about serving others. The fruit of our lives joined together in love was intended to be shared and to radiate outward, beginning with our children and extending to all those God would send us. We each belonged first and foremost to God, and that required generosity—a willingness to joyfully share each another, as well as our time, energy, talents, and possessions with others.

Almost two years into married life, as we excitedly scraped together money for our very first (and current) home, we sensed that God was calling us to a life of hospitality and generosity.

The practical reality of this wasn't always easy. I didn't always do it with ease and joy, especially as Peter traveled often when our kids were young, and our relatives didn't live nearby to help. But throughout the years we have tried to heed God's call to feed the hungry and welcome the stranger, the lonely, and the afflicted. We've hosted countless youth meetings, parties, Bible studies, prayer rooms, and guests from all over the world. We've cooked food for the homeless, made care packages for the poor, tithed generously, and invited others to live with us. In addition to our "open door policy," Peter has always valued my ministry endeavors outside the home. His support has enabled me to direct a week-long middle school camp every summer of our married life and lead a ministry for young women. At times, all of this meant that our life was messier, noisier, and less planned than I naturally would have preferred. But growing in the virtue of generosity has taught Peter and me to trust God for His care and provision in all things. It has also helped our children learn how to share, live more selflessly, and open their hearts to those in need.

A humorous incident from a few years ago sums up this way of generosity. Peter and I had settled in for a quiet Friday night alone when a car with an out-of-state license plate pulled into our driveway and a couple rang our doorbell. I had no idea who they were or why they were standing on our front step with suitcases. Peter looked panicked; not only had he forgotten to tell me about their visit; he didn't remember they were coming! Like other times, we put more pasta on the stove, prepared the guest room, and later laughed about our need for better communication.

Over the years, in different seasons of life, through trial and error, give and take, and lots of communication, we've learned how to share our lives with others. As our children grew and their activities increased, we regularly reassessed how to better balance our time commitments to ministry jobs, community, and each other and how to protect our family time and create appropriate boundaries in our home. There is tremendous freedom and joy in not trying to possess other people or our material goods but viewing everything as belonging to God—as gifts to be cherished and shared with others. As we have practiced generosity, we have discovered that we can never outdo God in generosity, for it is in giving that we receive.

Lesson #2: Love Covers a Multitude of Sins

Living under the Lordship of Jesus means we seek to please Him. We do this by obeying Him, despite the way we feel. One of the most important aspects of maintaining a life of love in the home is the area of forgiveness. In any healthy relationship there will consistently be five words spoken. The first three are: "I love you" and the last two are: "Forgive me." The people we love the most are imperfect, which means that despite their best efforts and intentions, they will fail and disappoint us in many ways (as we will them).

Even when we encounter one another's failures, weaknesses, and annoying habits, we are commanded to practice mercy and forgiveness. Why? Because this is how God relates to us. "As a father has compassion on his children, so the Lord has compassion on those who fear him; for he knows how we are formed, he remembers that we are dust" (Ps 103:13–14 NIV). The sins and weaknesses of those we love—and our own—should never surprise us because we are human. This reality should never justify our actions, but it should fill us with humility and tenderhearted compassion toward ourselves and one another.

> Therefore, as God's chosen people, holy and dearly loved, clothe yourselves with compassion, kindness, humility, gentleness and patience. Bear with each other and forgive one another if any of

you has a grievance against someone. Forgive as the Lord forgave you. And over all these virtues put on love, which binds them all together in perfect unity. (Col 3:12–14 NIV)

Life within a family presents infinite opportunities to practice forbearance, compassion, and godly love. As a husband and father, I've learned how to express patient love by refraining from nagging, letting go of little things, and not keeping score so that resentment cannot grow. It means loving unconditionally as Christ loves, not *when* you empty the dishwasher, or *if* you listen attentively to me, or *until* you hurt my feelings. When we are offended, our human tendency is to close ourselves off or strike back as a form of self-protection. But Jesus tells us that it is hardness of heart, more than failure, that can damage our relationship with God and others (Matt 19:18).

Marriage and family life have given us at least "seventy times seven" opportunities to practice forgiveness (Matt 18:22). There will always be hurt in close relationships that inevitably comes from selfishness, misunderstandings, a lack of charity, and a loss of trust. Forgiveness doesn't excuse or condone the wrong done to us, but it allows us to say, "I no longer want this hurt to control my life, I do not want it to define who I am or will become. I don't want it to grow into bitterness and resentment. I want to be free." Forgiveness means refusing to make someone pay for what they did, even if they deserve it.

Often the most difficult part of forgiving another is facing the fact that we don't actually *want* to forgive them. Yet the process of forgiveness also requires that we experience, within ourselves, the fact that we are not so different from those we are so ready to judge. We must forgive because God has forgiven the inexcusable in us. There is no sin or wound that forgiveness cannot heal. Learning to freely ask for and extend forgiveness is a powerful key to freedom and healing. When we were dating and throughout our marriage, we practiced forgiveness and also taught our children at a young age how to forgive us and one another.

I remember a vivid example when our boys were in late elementary school and early junior high. One night past their bedtime, the boys (who shared a room in the basement), were still making a lot of noise. I went downstairs twice, firmly reminding them it was time to be quiet and go to bed. After several minutes, it was clear they hadn't calmed down, so, angry and frustrated, I headed downstairs for the third time. I yelled at them, shoved a desk chair across the room, turned off the lights, slammed the door, and stomped out. A few minutes later as we were getting ready for bed, Debbie suggested that I check on the boys and bring some closure to the situation. I stubbornly pointed out that my actions were justified by the boys' disobedience. I think I said something profound like, "It's their problem. They had it coming." But as I lay in bed, I realized that this was a learning moment for me and my boys. It was an opportunity for me to walk in the footsteps of Jesus by leading as a father the way He would want me to do. So, I went back downstairs and brought the boys into another room for a chat. It was clear they were a bit shaken and angry with me. I told them that it was okay to be mad, but Scripture tells us to be angry but not to sin, and I had clearly crossed that line by losing control of my temper (Eph 4:26). I asked each of them to forgive me for the way I behaved and told them I didn't want to do it again because it wasn't pleasing to the Lord. They were hesitant; they didn't want to forgive me. I acknowledged their feelings and told them that forgiveness is ultimately a decision—not a feeling—to obey and trust Jesus. I led them in the correct way to extend forgiveness and instead of just saying, "It doesn't matter," or "It's okay," they were able to say, "Dad, I forgive you for what you did." The boys also asked my forgiveness (with a little help from me) for not obeying me in the first place. We exchanged a hug, I told them I loved them, and we went to bed.

This instance of forgiveness, and many others, underlined important principles for our family. All of us have the same responsibility before the Lord—both to obey Him and to protect our family relationships. I wasn't only trying to follow a rule, but I was making every effort to keep the unity of the Spirit through the bond of peace and to reflect to my children the merciful and loving heart of their heavenly Father (Eph 4:3).

Lesson #3: We Are Earthen Vessels

> *"But we have this treasure in earthen vessels (clay jars), so that it may be made clear that this extraordinary power belongs to God and does not come from us."* (2 Cor 4:7)

We have already spent some time talking about the Treasure, who is the Holy Trinity, the One who is Love, who created us in love for love. We reflect the reality of this treasure in the marriage relationship and in the fruit of our unitive love (our children). Marriage is intended to be an image of the absolute and unfailing love of God for the human race and a reflection of the love between the divine Persons of the Trinity.

But marriage, because it is lived in the context of our humanity, also reveals to us how much we are earthen vessels! Very few of us awake each morning, roll over, look at our spouse, and think (or say): "Good morning dear treasure, today I am going to do everything I can to esteem, value, affirm, protect, preserve, honor, and love you." Instead, at the end of a long day many of us are worn out, discouraged, and irritable; the shine on the treasure seems to have faded a bit. We often fail to recognize the invaluable treasure that has been entrusted to us because what we mainly see is an earthen vessel, a jar of clay, a cracked pot. The reality of how weak, wounded, and broken we are as humans can be discouraging and disheartening, making us want to hide or even give up sometimes. But if we are rooted in faith and persevere in love, we can meet our own brokenness and that of our spouse with courage. We can draw hope from the reality that the most beautiful treasure in the universe came to us in an earthen vessel. God the Creator sent His Son to become a dependent creature who was ignored, rejected, misunderstood, and silenced. He freely allowed His body to be broken, bruised, whipped, wounded, and crucified to show us what true love looks like.

In the school of love, we step into risk, messiness, and brokenness so that we learn a deeper kind of love that emerges from dependence and trust. The way of the world says, "If your earthen vessel has lost its shine, find another one—tighter face, a more toned body, a new wardrobe, a different spouse!" But the world's treasure is a cheap counterfeit. The way of God is weakness, dependence, humility, and vulnerability. It means allowing our spouse to get very close—to truly see, know, and love us even when we believe there is nothing in us that is lovable or desirable. In the school of love, we allow ourselves to be broken and poured out in love, even when it doesn't seem to be reciprocated or appreciated. In doing so, it allows God to fill our clay jar with His fullness and truly shine through us a glorious reflection of His powerful and transformative love. This type of love is not easily learned and comes at a cost. But the alternative to not risking, as C. S. Lewis articulates, is even more frightening.

> To love at all is to be vulnerable. Love anything and your heart will be wrung and possibly broken. If you want to make sure of keeping it intact you must give it to no one, not even an animal. Wrap it carefully round with hobbies and little luxuries; avoid all entanglements. Lock it up safe in the casket or coffin of your selfishness. But in that casket, safe, dark, motionless, airless, it will change. It will not be broken; it will become unbreakable, impenetrable, irredeemable.[6]

Marriage, more than any other relationship, requires this deep level of vulnerability. Intimacy happens over time as we open our thoughts, wounds, and weaknesses to each other and allow our spouse into the places that feel risky, messy, and impossible to change. The fruit of vulnerability in marriage is deeper love expressed in emotional and physical intimacy.

Peter and I both grew up in dysfunctional families, and there are areas of pain and trauma that have

---

[6] C. S. Lewis, *The Four Loves* (New York: Harcourt Brace Modern Classic, 1960), 121.

often hindered vulnerability and intimacy in our marriage. Early on in our marriage, we didn't pay enough attention to the reasons we lacked emotional health. In many daily ways we loved each other well, and together we loved Jesus, our family, and others. But we allowed the busyness of family life to be an unspoken reason for avoiding the painful acknowledgment and necessary healing that leads to vulnerability and deeper love. If you are married, it is as true for you as it is for us: *nothing will change in your marriage if each person isn't willing to change.* As difficult as it is to change ourselves, it is impossible to change another person. We must learn to accept and welcome others as they are, not as we want them to be. Our effort is to change ourselves, not others, and to ask for the grace to see others as Christ sees them—with hope and love. God wants to give each of us the quality of meekness, the ability to endure injury with patience and without resentment. This doesn't mean being spineless or lacking in courage; it means to be like Christ and to exhibit strength under control (Matt 11:29).

It is an act of love for yourself and your spouse to address your own issues and, when necessary, to get the help to do so. When we do this, we find that areas of pain become the means of deeper healing, growth, and love. This often takes time, and we must learn how to live in the tension of our human messiness and the Divine Healer's work of restoration. Our goal isn't to create the illusion of perfection to ourselves or the outside world but to love God and one another in the midst of our imperfections. With St. Paul, we can say, "I do not consider myself yet to have taken hold of it. But one thing I do: Forgetting what is behind and straining toward what is ahead, I press on toward the goal to win the prize for which God has called me heavenward in Christ Jesus"

(Phil 3:13–14 NIV). Although we are all still a work in progress, we press on in hope, striving to love ourselves, our spouse, our family, and others the way our heavenly Father loves us.

The person God loves with a tenderness of a Father, the person He wants to touch and transform with His love, is not the person we'd have liked to be or ought to be. It's the person we are. God doesn't love "ideal persons" or "virtual beings." He loves actual, real people.[7]

The good news is that we are never alone. Through the sacrament of marriage, Christ is with us. And when we actively and intentionally put Him at the center of our relationship, He is our refuge and strength, a very present help in trouble (Ps 46:1), and in all these things we are more than conquerors through Him who loved us (Rom 8:37), because what is impossible with man is possible with God (Luke 18:27).

---

[7] Jacques Philippe, *Interior Freedom* (Strongsville, OH: Scepter Publishers, 2007) 32.

Chapter 4

BUILDING OUR WAY OF LIFE

When we were first approached about writing a book on marriage and family life, my initial response was, "Thank you for the opportunity, but no." I was hesitant, acutely aware of the mistakes that Debbie and I have made along the way. Each family, like every person, is unique, unrepeatable, and complex. Each has its own constellation of strengths and weaknesses, virtues and vices, family histories, personality types, dysfunctions, natural and spiritual gifts, and relational capacities. There isn't any one-size-fits-all formula for building a healthy, Christ-centered family life. But in our role as parents, grandparents, and mentors for young adults, we recognize the need for practical wisdom in a world that is increasingly challenging and often hostile to a Christian worldview.

In this chapter, we want to share with you some of the habits of thinking and the practical decisions that helped us build our own family culture. To begin with, we knew that we did not possess the power on our own to create the kind of family life we most wanted, one that was centered on the person of Jesus. Jesus states this clearly to His Apostles: "He who abides in me, and I in him, he it is that bears much fruit, *for apart from me you can do nothing*" (John 15:5). That simple truth was foundational for us. We knew our best intentions, strength of will, personal creativity, and commitment were not enough. Christian family life is not simply a human construct that is the result of effort alone. Family life is a natural reality. Christian family life is a supernatural reality; it's a miracle, brought about by the interworking of God's grace and our efforts to respond to His power.

Christian family life is built on the grace of the Sacrament of Matrimony. It is founded on a covenant between three persons: husband, wife, and God. It is that bond and the outworking of the promises of these three persons that makes it possible. Ultimately, Christian family is a place where God dwells. Christian family life is lived in and through Christ. It is natural in every way—ordinary, messy, and hard, but it is also animated by the presence and power of the Holy Spirit. That may sound a bit too lofty, but it was a big help and a bit of a relief for us to realize that we couldn't just make this happen on our own. We were aspiring to a way of life that was beyond us, especially given our weak, sinful natures. Understanding that fact, and knowing that God promised to be with us, that He was "all in," gave us genuine hope that it was possible. In fact, it created a sense of high adventure.

Abide in Me

Based on this understanding, with the encouragement of wise mentors, Debbie and I made the decision to commit to praying daily, just as we had before marriage. Friends told us that our marriage and our hopes for a family life centered on Jesus depended completely on our individual, daily commitment to spending quality time with the Lord. Put simply, our goal was to build a way of life that expressed the life of Jesus. That way of life is the fruit that comes from abiding in Him, and the foundation and power source of abiding is prayer. This means talking to Jesus from the heart daily: reading His word, accepting His promises, asking for His help, obeying His commands, and following His leadership. Prayer is the lifeline that connects us individually and corporately to Jesus, who is the life source of a Christian marriage and family.

That decision has been the cornerstone of our married life. It required a personal commitment on both our parts to help one another find time each day for prayer. It's true that we can talk with Jesus throughout the day, but if we want to grow in our relationship with Him, a daily time of undisturbed prayer is necessary. Depending on what stage of life your family is in, this will require teamwork. In the early years of our marriage when the children were small, I would take my prayer time before everyone else woke up. Then I would help the kids get ready for the day while Debbie took her prayer time. As you might guess, it wasn't perfect every day, but we worked at trying to make it happen! Christ-centered family life flows from the parents' commitment to prayer, from each individual's personal communion and relationship with Jesus. Parents cannot give what they do not have nor lead their children into a way of life that they are not living. They cannot teach their children what it means to have a relationship with Jesus if they don't have one themselves.

The Lord's Day

Another very important decision we made was to keep the Lord's Day holy and make it special, which included as its most important element the non-negotiable family attendance at weekly Sunday Mass. That meant, other than sickness, nothing took precedence over going to Mass together. As our children entered high school, Mass attendance was still required, and we placed a high priority on going as a family.

For many years, we observed the Lord's Day by setting aside twenty-four hours, from dinner Saturday night to dinner on Sunday. After a typical Saturday of activities—chores, kids' athletics, or watching college football, the Lord's Day began with prayers and customs adapted from Debbie's Jewish upbringing. We welcomed the Sabbath with the lighting of a candle and the blessing of challah bread, followed by a nicer celebrative meal. We often invited other families or single people to join us. After the meal, we would all help with dishes, sing songs, play games, visit with friends, and occasionally watch a good movie. We did our best to keep out all the typical distractions and guard this precious time together. As our kids' lives got busier throughout high school with academics, theater, sports, and social activities, it was no longer realistic to celebrate the Lord's Day together every Saturday evening, but we maintained aspects of it throughout the year and the kids often invited their friends to join us.

On Sunday after Mass we sometimes invited guests for brunch, played games, went on walks, visited other families, napped, and did our best to avoid work, shopping, and chores. Our main goal was to honor the Lord's Day as a family and to rest from the hectic pace of activities. This was an important way to unplug from the wider secular culture that no longer values the Lord's Day. There were many important lessons our children learned through this family ritual: the importance of obedience to the commandments of the Lord, the willingness to be different, the centrality of worship, the duty we owe to God, the need for quiet and rest, the value of family, friendships in the Lord, the cost of discipleship, and most important, the central role the Holy Eucharist plays in the formation of God's people. Debbie and I did our best to communicate to our children that we considered the Mass and the Lord's Day the high point of our week. We weren't dragging ourselves to Mass simply out of obligation. There were days when the kids grumbled and complained, especially during teen years, but for the most part, they embraced our approach.

The teen years presented more complexities and other good activities competed for their time and threatened to conflict with our family values. One of the most common family challenges are sports schedules. One of our boys played Amateur Athletic Union basketball in the summers throughout high school, which included regional and sometimes national travel. Games were typically all day Saturday and into Sunday, with the championship game often extending into early afternoon. Each year we made it clear to our son and his coaches before he joined the team that if there was a schedule conflict between a game—even if it was the championship game—and it was the only time he could get to Mass in the city in which they were playing, Mass always came first. Every coach respected our decision. It wasn't always easy, but we managed during all those years of competitive sports to never miss a Sunday Mass. It's a great joy now to see that all four of our adult children—three raising their own families—have integrated the celebration of the Lord's Day, Mass, and Sunday rest into their own lives.

Family Dinner

Dinners were some of the most important and formative times we shared together as a family. Over the years, Debbie and I put a lot of thought into making the most of mealtimes. It was a laboratory in which we would test ideas we came up with or borrowed from others on how to engage our children in age-specific spiritual conversations. Of course, most of dinner was just eating, telling stories about the day, trying to keep the little ones in their seats, refereeing arguments about doing the dishes, checking in on homework, and coordinating carpools and schedules. We ate our meals together around our table with no phones, computers, or television present. We worked hard to guard the dinner hour, and we tried to say no to activities that occurred during that time. Family dinner ended when all the dishes and meal clean-up was finished—chores that included everyone's help!

Family Prayer

Amidst the normal chaos and unpredictability of the dinner hour, in addition to the traditional blessing before the meal, we made strategic use of the time we had to pray together. When the children were little, we would read age-appropriate Bible stories and sing, and as they got older, we would share the daily Gospel reading. During the teen years, we would often have family prayer at 9:00 p.m. when we could gather (and even our dog was present!) for the Rosary and intercessory prayer before bedtime. At times when the kids' friends were at the house hanging out, they would also join us for night prayers, because that's what the Herbeck family did.

Tradition!

It is so important as a family to celebrate life together—birthdays, weddings, holy days, sacraments, the first day of school, graduations, births, and even deaths—in ways that are special and unique to each family culture. Peter and I brought different family customs into our marriage that were meaningful. Even before we were married, we discussed how we could observe and integrate those traditions into our family life. I grew up in a Jewish home and it is important to me that our children have a strong identification with their Jewish heritage through the celebration of the Jewish holidays. For thirty-six years, we have conducted a Passover Seder in our home, celebrated the Festival of Hanukkah with the lighting of the menorah and gift giving, and observed Rosh Hashana (Jewish New Year) and Yom Kippur (Day of Atonement). These celebrations with special prayers, foods, and preparation require more work, but they have been significant in helping our children not only identify with their Jewish roots, but also understand the continuity and fulfillment of the Old Testament in Jesus the Messiah and in the New Israel, the Church.

We also took great care to develop our own Herbeck family faith traditions. We observed within our home the major seasons of the liturgical year like Advent and Lent with candle lighting, special prayers, and symbols like an Advent wreath and calendar, a bowl of ashes on the table, simpler meals, and almsgiving. Christmas, Epiphany, Pentecost, and other feast days were also celebrated with the intentionality of honoring the Lord and helping our children understand their faith. All these visible elements were signs and physical reminders of deeper spiritual realities. For years our family attended our parish Easter Vigil, which began at sundown and lasted three to four hours. After six weeks of Lenten sacrifices, our kids loved this Mass in the darkened, candle lit church, with its stirring music and the growing anticipation of the celebration of the Resurrection.

Watching our adult children begin to develop their own faith cultures within their growing families reminds us of how challenging yet valuable it is to do so. Incorporating consistent spiritual practices like prayer, Scripture readings, and focused spiritual discussions takes time, effort, creativity, and discernment as a couple in order to engage kids at various ages. Don't despise small beginnings or give up when it is frustrating or seems to bear little fruit. If you persevere, it signals to the family that prayer is important and nonnegotiable, and a rhythm of life together will emerge.

Teamwork

Early on in our marriage we received some great advice about the importance of a weekly husband and wife meeting. It wasn't a date night (which we also highly recommend), but a practical meeting for about ninety minutes. The point of the meeting is to communicate about important personal and practical things that can help us "maintain a spirit of unity in the bond of peace" (Eph 4:3) in our relationship and in our home.

At first, the idea of another regular weekly meeting in our already busy schedules wasn't an attractive prospect, and it sounded too bureaucratic. But in the end, it turned out to be quite helpful. The meeting had a simple agenda. We focused on several key questions. First, "How are you doing personally?" Work and kids didn't usually give us a lot of spontaneous time to discuss the emotional, spiritual, and relational aspects of our life. This meeting gave us a place to communicate regularly and to avoid a buildup of unspoken and unresolved problems, which can easily lead to a house divided.

The second question we tackled was "How are the kids doing?" Taking time to talk about each one of our four children helped us form a common strategy on how to best parent each one of them. We learned through discussion how to identify our parenting strengths and weaknesses and to "tag team" in our parenting styles, especially as the kids got older and needed different things from each of us. I found these discussions particularly helpful because often Debbie would have a better pulse on how the kids were doing. We didn't always agree on the best approach, but we knew that presenting a united front was necessary for both our marriage and our children.

In every family, there is pain and struggle at times. Kids go through difficult phases, and as parents it's not always easy to know what to do. Looking back, some of the most challenging times were the most rewarding for us as a couple. We would normally pray a decade of the Rosary for each of the kids, and other times we would simply be on our knees crying out to God for guidance and grace for the child or children who were having the hardest time. We received so much help from the Lord—encouragement, wisdom, and timely insight from the Holy Spirit, which helped us fight fear and produced hope.

The third question we discussed at this meeting was the most practical: "What's on the schedule this week?" Family life is busy, filled with lots of details that need to be coordinated in advance to maintain the peace. More than anything we did as a couple, that meeting consistently helped us work together in this humbling but exciting adventure of building a family culture around the Person of Jesus.

Our desire to shape our life according to God's purpose required balance. It meant we didn't try to control all the outcomes, but we didn't just let life happen either. Debbie's temperament is more laid back, and I am more intense. Sometimes my ideas are great, but not realistic for our family, and sometimes Debbie needs to be pushed outside her comfort zone. In all of it, together we are a team.

Chapter 5

MISSION POSSIBLE: HELPING OUR CHILDREN ENCOUNTER CHRIST

There have been so many important and poignant "firsts" in our children's lives, but some of the ones I, Debbie, recall the most were about "coming home." I remember the first time Sarah, our eldest, walked home alone from the corner bus stop in first grade, and when she got her driver's license, and a week later her first car accident when she was rear-ended turning onto our street. I remember when Michael made his first twelve-hour road trip home from college and when Rachel flew home after a semester in Rome. I remember waiting at the baggage claim for Josh to come home after his first deployment in the army. In all these circumstances and more, all I could think of was wanting them *home*, safe and sound.

As parents, we have many plans and desires for our children, but God our Father has only one ultimate goal: *to get every beloved son and daughter safely home, to live with Him in heaven for eternity.* It is easy to lose sight of this supreme goal amidst the pressing demands of life, and especially within a predominantly secular culture that is increasingly averse to a Christian worldview and an eternal perspective. But nothing else is more important to our Lord, and ultimately nothing else should be more important to us.

The Church exists to evangelize—it is her deepest identity, and her mission is to make disciples. The family is described as the domestic Church because it is the first place where young, baptized Christians learn about their faith. "In it parents should, by their word and example, be the first preachers of the faith to their children."[1] Every domestic Church has a mission and a responsibility right within the family to make disciples and thus lead souls to heaven. The biblical understanding of a disciple is someone who follows Jesus, learns from Jesus, and conforms his or her life to the words and ways of Jesus. A mature disciple makes a conscious, firm decision, carried out in action, to be a follower of Jesus Christ no matter the cost to oneself.[2]

Although Peter and I have been actively involved in ministry and evangelization in the Church our whole married life, we recognized early on that our mission begins at home, that our own family is our primary field of evangelization. We understood that we weren't just raising our children to be responsible citizens or good people. Our intention was to help them become disciples and saints. Quite honestly, at times we had to fight hard to keep our focus and efforts there. I remember times as a young mother when I struggled to balance the hiddenness

---

[1] Second Vatican Council, Dogmatic Constitution on the Church *Lumen Gentium* (November 21, 1964), § 11.
[2] National Conference of Catholic Bishops, *A Pastoral Letter on Stewardship*, November 1992.

of home life and a desire to be "doing more for God." One day in prayer, Jesus spoke clearly to my heart: "If you evangelize the whole world, and you have not done your part to help your own children know Me, you have not fulfilled your vocation as their mother." There were also times when Peter decided to cut back on travel in order to be more present and available to us.

An inspirational model that reminds us of our role as parents is St. John the Baptist. He was never confused or distracted from his primary purpose: to prepare the way of the Lord (Matt 3:3). Our family life must be a highway for our God—a place we prepare for the coming of the Lord, where He dwells and where faith is living and active. We must proclaim and teach God's truth to our children with clarity. Today, in our postmodern culture where religion is no longer considered the single defining source of truth and reality, this requires courage and conviction, especially when we feel like John the Baptist—a lone voice crying out in the wilderness. Although the culture is changing rapidly, the current condition of our world was prophetically articulated and assessed by Pope Benedict more than twenty years ago:

> In our days, when in vast areas of the world the faith is in danger of dying out like a flame which no longer has fuel, the overriding priority is to make God present in this world and to show men and women the way to God. . . . The real problem at this moment of our history is that God is disappearing from the human horizon, and, with the dimming of the light which comes

from God, humanity is losing its bearings, with increasingly evident destructive effects.[3]

Currently, the culture is shaping the next generation's understanding of the faith far more than their faith is shaping their understanding of the culture. As the mother of four adult children and grandmother of ten little ones, and with forty years of youth ministry under my belt, I believe with great conviction and urgency that if we aren't intentionally and actively helping our kids know and love Jesus personally, the secular world with its radicalized relativism and individualism will eagerly take our place as the loudest and most influential voice in their lives.

The call to evangelize our children can seem daunting and we often feel ill equipped. It takes a plan and an understanding of what is needed to help our children at various ages encounter Christ and grow in their personal relationship with Him. It requires determination and perseverance to execute that plan together as parents. But we must also remember that it doesn't just depend on our schemes and efforts; there is no foolproof formula for raising holy kids. We are cooperating with God's grace in their lives and our "work" includes praying for them, asking the Holy Spirit to give us wisdom, and entrusting them to His merciful love. Without prayer, our human efforts are limited, and we can easily fall prey to discouragement and fear.

A part of Peter's conversion that touches me so deeply is the story he tells about his own mother and the power of prayer. He has many childhood memories of seeing

---

[3] Pope Benedict XVI, *Letter Concerning the Remission of the Excommunication of the Four Bishops Consecrated by Archbishop Lefebvre* (March 10, 2009).

his mom praying the Rosary daily in her chair in the den and seeing her kneeling by her bed in prayer when he snuck in late at night during his wayward teenage years. The eternal destiny of her seven children and her beloved alcoholic husband weighed heavily on her heart, and she brought each one to the Lord and to His Mother daily. When Peter had a dramatic conversion experience at a large Catholic conference in Notre Dame's football stadium, it was his mom who greeted him as he arrived home in the early morning. They stood in the kitchen together, and as Peter searched for the words to describe that life-changing personal encounter, he began to cry. His diminutive mom wrapped her arms around her teenage son and said, "Peter, you don't have to explain. I've prayed for this your whole life!" Dorothy Herbeck's perseverance in daily intercessory prayer for her family bore great fruit. Today, many of her seventy-three children, grandchildren, and great grandchildren are living for the Lord. At age ninety-three, her prized rosary was handed on, and she took her place among the great cloud of witnesses who are interceding and cheering us Home.

Teach the Faith

There are three primary ways parents can help lead their children into a life of discipleship and love. The first way is to teach the faith. As the primary teachers of their children, parents impart knowledge of the faith and help them acquire values and virtues necessary for Christian living.

Scripture prioritizes teaching as one of the primary methods of helping future generations know Christ and grow in maturity.

> *He commanded our fathers to teach . . . their children; that the next generation might know them, the children yet unborn, and arise and tell them to their children. (Ps 78:5–6)*
>
> *Hear, my son, your father's instruction, and reject not your mother's teaching. (Prov 1:8)*
>
> *Fathers, do not provoke your children to anger, but bring them up in the discipline and instruction of the Lord. (Eph 6:4)*

As children get older, it can be easy to abdicate our educational responsibilities to "trained experts" and rely entirely on Catholic school education, parish catechesis, and youth groups.

Education in the faith by the parents should begin in the child's earliest years. This already happens when family members help one another to grow in faith by the witness of a Christian life in keeping with the Gospel. "Family catechesis precedes, accompanies, and enriches other forms of instruction in the faith" (CCC 2226).

Parents must take the lead and, with the help of clergy, catechists, teachers, godparents, and Confirmation sponsors, communicate the truths of the faith in a credible way. This entails more than just reiterating doctrine or setting down rules but helping them understand the faith through stories and questions. Because our culture lacks a coherent story about the meaning and purpose of life, kids must know Christianity as the true story of all reality as revealed in Scripture as *their own story*, not just a list of beliefs, rules, or historical facts.[4]

In our family, we read Bible stories and the lives of the saints to our younger kids and as they got older, we followed the Church's daily readings as part of our family prayer. We wove the traditions of my Jewish heritage with the Church's liturgical year, communicating God's plan of salvation and its fulfillment in the Incarnation, death, and Resurrection of Jesus the Messiah to our children through celebration, prayer, food, stories, and liturgy. Some of our most cherished times were sitting around our dining room table each Passover and Easter as our children recounted the story of God's deliverance of Israel from Egypt, and they began to understand that Jesus was the spotless Lamb that was slain for our sins.

Parents must also create space for kids to ask difficult questions about life, God, and faith. As children enter adolescence, a time of questioning and pushing boundaries is normal as they move from a childhood faith and identification with their family's beliefs to making faith their own. Children naturally need more independence and freedom as they grow into adolescence, but they also need consistent guidelines and ongoing formation. It can be difficult to find the right balance between the two. Especially as our kids got older, we tried not to just dispense rules but to help them understand through discussion the reasons behind our approach and eventually take personal ownership. Culture, media, and technology are so loud and prevalent right now that for many young people it is their primary (and quite unreliable) source of

---

[4] John Stonestreet and Brett Kunkle, *A Practical Guide to Culture: Helping the Next Generation Navigate Today's World* (Colorado Springs, CO: David C. Cook, 2020), 107.

information and formation. It is alarming to see twelve- and thirteen-year-olds post and repost on social media their opinions on social issues about which they know very little.

Young people need trusted adults who can help them find answers and deal with real-life issues. This means giving them permission to question, wrestle, and be honest with God and themselves. These opportunities for questioning teach kids to think critically about the faith, to understand what the Church teaches, what they believe and *why* they are living it, so they can confidently meet the challenges of teenage years and young adulthood. The goal isn't to just tell them *what* to think, but to teach them *how* to think, how to discern what is true, and to make good decisions not based on cultural norms or their feelings but on God's truth. Some kids are more naturally compliant, while others question and challenge. But deeper conversion and discipleship for our children cannot happen if they are only given information about the faith. They need parents and mentors to walk with them on their faith journey—through their questions, struggles, doubts, apathy, discoveries, and growth.

See the Faith

My (Debbie's) father used to tell us jokingly when we were kids: "Do as I say, not as I do!" Our children will rarely follow our instruction if we are only demanding it from them but not living it ourselves. One of the first and most effective means of evangelization is the witness of an authentically Christian life.[5] We profess faith in God and set an example in our home by consistently

---

[5] Pope Paul VI, Apostolic Exhortation *Evangelii Nuntiandi* (December 8, 1975).

and joyfully acting according to the Gospel. Creating a Christ-centered environment and a family culture that reflects Gospel values and then adhering to our way of life sent an important message to our children. We didn't always live it perfectly, but they knew the Catholic faith was our foundational and most important identity, and we weren't making it up as we went along or shaping our life according to the latest trends.

We made some intentional family decisions to cultivate faith and the virtues of sacrifice, self-control, generosity, gratitude, prudence, purity, love, and respect. We didn't give our children everything they wanted or what everyone else had. We had clear expectations for behavior that we enforced with clear consequences for disobedience. During Lent, we practiced almsgiving and taught our kids at an early age to give some of their clothing and toys to the less fortunate, made meals for the homeless, and opened our home to others. Each birthday was celebrated with a favorite meal and a time of honoring. Although it was awkward at times, our children learned the importance of expressing appreciation and honor to others.

As the kids grew, we limited television time; monitored music, media, and social situations; discouraged dating relationships; collected phones at bedtime; and used web filters on our family computer to teach prudence, chastity, modesty, and self-control. I'm sure there were times when our kids thought they were the only ones not allowed to see a particular movie or listen to certain types of music! Peter and I tried to model speech that was patient, loving, and respectful, and we tried to live our faith as authentically and consistently as possible.

We found that over time it was (and still is) the steady, daily commitments to Christ and one another that allow our children to see and experience the treasure of our faith most profoundly. Faithful married love, meals together, daily prayer, being present to our kids, facing the suffering of miscarriages, illness, and family deaths together with hope is the glue that holds our family together in Christ.

A few years ago, someone asked our oldest daughter to identify one of the factors that impacted her faith life as she was growing up. Her response was seeing her dad each morning in the living room taking time to pray and read Scripture. We may not always see the immediate effects of our actions, but we can't underestimate the impact of small acts of love and fidelity to Jesus. A friend of mine took her freshman daughter to college and a few weeks into the semester her daughter called to say, "Thank you for the example of going to daily Mass when I was growing up, because now that I'm on my own, I know where and how to find my strength."

> Parents have the first responsibility for the education of their children. They bear witness to this responsibility first by creating a home where tenderness, forgiveness, respect, fidelity, and disinterested service are the rule. The home is well suited for education in the virtues. . . . Parents have a grave responsibility to give good example to their children. By knowing how to acknowledge their own failings to their children, parents will be better able to guide and correct them. (CCC 2223)

Being an authentic witness doesn't mean we do it perfectly. It's beautiful and rewarding when children imitate our virtuous actions but also terrifying to see them imitate our flaws and mistakes. I remember years ago at Mass, during the Consecration, a small voice from a pew shouted for all of us to hear: "I thought you told us not to say shut up!" We've all had times with our children—some more humorous than others—when their words and actions seem to broadcast our faults and weaknesses, and we are sure that we are failing as parents. Yet if we walk in humility, our deficiencies, imperfections, and failures can be opportunities for repentance, forgiveness, restoration, growth, and holiness—for ourselves and our children!

The African proverb that "it takes a village to raise a child" is certainly true in helping our children "see the faith." We knew we needed other faith-filled people to reinforce and support our efforts, and so we cultivated relationships with families who shared our values. We invited into our life "normal" and relatable young adults who lived their faith with passion and conviction. Frequent guests—bishops, priests, and lay people from Africa, Canada, Eastern Europe, China, the Middle East, as well as musicians, athletes, young couples, and college students exemplified the beautiful mosaic of the Catholic Church to our family.

Ultimately, we found that our kids' happiness didn't depend on more stuff or better extracurricular activities. They needed their parents and the adults in their lives to be present and to value the pursuit of holiness over comfort and self-indulgence. Our children learned through experience that God is trustworthy, there is joy in following Him, and that His way is better than ours.

Personal Encounter

As parents we want to ensure that our kids understand their faith as more than a set of beliefs and behaviors. Helping them develop a well-formed conscience is very important, but just knowing right from wrong is not enough. Christianity isn't just about how to behave; it's about our identity—who we are as God's beloved children. Our children need to know not just what to stay away from but what, or more precisely *who*, to live for. This means it is necessary for parents to help facilitate an encounter with the Person of Jesus.

Our relationship with Jesus is personal but never private, compartmentalized, or lived in isolation from others—especially our children. Jesus isn't just Mom and Dad's friend, the boss of our ministry, something we do, somewhere we go on Sundays. The Resurrection isn't just a historical event we celebrate at Easter but an invitation to the life and power of God. Introducing our children to the concept of a personal relationship with Jesus begins at an early age with how we speak about God, how we address Him in prayer, and how we express our love for Him and for others. We call Him Father, Friend, Savior, and Redeemer. He desires every person, young or old, to come into a personal, life-changing relationship with the Father, Son, and Holy Spirit. The recent Popes have underlined the importance of this personal encounter with Jesus.

> Sometimes even Catholics have lost or never had the chance to experience Christ personally: not Christ as a mere "paradigm" or "value," but as

the living Lord, "the way, and the truth, and the life."[6] (Pope St. John Paul II)

Christianity is not an intellectual system, a collection of dogmas, or a moralism. Christianity is an encounter, a love story; it is an event.[7] (Pope Emeritus Benedict XVI)

May the Lord give us the grace, to encounter him but also to let ourselves be encountered by him. The beautiful grace of astonishment at the encounter, but also the grace of having the twofold confession in our life: "You are the Christ, the Son of the living God, I believe. And I am a sinner, I believe."[8] (Pope Francis)

At the heart of this encounter is not merely theoretical knowledge of God but something that is relational and experiential. In the Bible, to know God means not merely to know about Him but to have a relationship with Him—to have personal knowledge of His love and to experience His guidance, wisdom, and gifts—given to us in the Spirit through Baptism and Confirmation and developed in our lives as we walk in faith.

As our children entered junior high and high school, we helped them find peer environments where Christ was present, faith was alive, and they could grow in their faith and be challenged as leaders. Junior high camps, mission trips, mentors, youth conferences, retreats, small

---

[6] Pope St. John Paul II, *Address to the Bishops of the United States of America On Their "Ad Limina" Visit* (March 20, 1993).

[7] Joseph Ratzinger, "Homily for Funeral of Msgr. Luigi Giussani," *Communio* 31 (2004): 685.

[8] Pope Francis, *Homily*, Casa Santa Marta (September 3, 2015).

groups, and school retreats inspired deeper personal conversion, helped them take ownership of their faith, grow in confidence, and begin to lead others. As our kids began to form friendships with peers who were also serious about their faith, they shared a vision and a mission for their life that generated support and deeper conviction. Mission trips and service projects provided opportunities to "unplug" from technology and the stress of everyday life. Empowered to serve and help others, they were stretched outside their comfort zones, viewed their lives with a newfound appreciation, and had greater compassion for the less fortunate.

For us it wasn't about piling more activities onto our already full life. It meant making time and space for what was most important. It required an ongoing assessment of our priorities and motivations for each child. Did we primarily invest our time, money, and energy in the things that were helping them become better students, athletes, and musicians, or did we invest in those activities, events, and relationships that helped them know Jesus and grow in virtue? Some of our greatest joys have been serving alongside our children at camps, retreats, conferences, and mission trips. All our children (and their spouses) joined me as teenagers and young adults for a mission trip to the garbage dump in Mexico City, where we ministered to those who live and work there by providing basic medical care, food, clothing, and lots of love.

The seeds of faith and love of God that were sown in our family through our parish, schools, camps, and faith community took root and bore fruit in different ways and at different times in each of our children's lives. When young people encounter Christ's love, they begin to live in freedom and joy. Slowly, as their relationship with the

Lord grows and they mature, they care less about the opinions of others and more about honoring the Lord; they think less about themselves and more about others. They hunger after God and pray more; they serve willingly and selflessly and find ways to share God's love with others. It doesn't happen overnight; there are spiritual battles, setbacks, and growing pains. But I know it is possible, and I've witnessed disciples and saints in the making in our family and in many, many young people!

Programs and the transmission of information about the faith are not sufficient means to a personal encounter with Christ and a growing personal relationship with Him. Pope St. John Paul II articulated this so well when he said:

> We are certainly not seduced by the naïve expectation that, faced with the great challenges of our time, we shall find some magic formula. No, we shall not be saved by a formula but by a Person, and the assurance which he gives us: *I am with you!* It is not therefore a matter of inventing a "new programme." The programme already exists: it is the plan found in the Gospel and in the living Tradition, it is the same as ever. Ultimately, it has its center in Christ himself, who is to be known, loved and imitated, so that in him we may live the life of the Trinity, and with him transform history until its fulfilment in the heavenly Jerusalem.[9]

---

[9] Pope St. John Paul II Apostolic Letter at the Close of the Great Jubilee of the Year 2000 *Novo Millennio Ineunte* (January 6, 2001), § 29.

This seemingly impossible mission of raising disciples in our families is only possible through our cooperation with God's grace in our own lives. We want the very best for our children—true joy, lasting happiness, freedom, and life with God. But it's difficult to help our children find these things if we as parents haven't encountered God in our own lives. St. Teresa of Calcutta wrote a letter to her community giving the Missionaries of Charity the key to their vocation. So, too, it instructs us in our vocation as parents.

> I worry that some of you still haven't really met Jesus. One to one. You and him alone. Jesus wants me to tell you again, how much is the love He has for each one of you—beyond all that you can imagine. . . . Do you really know the living Jesus—not from books, but from being with Him in your heart? Have you heard the loving words He speaks to you? . . . Never give up on this daily intimate contact with Jesus as a real living person—not just an idea.[10]

We must challenge ourselves and one another to live the faith passionately, consistently, and faithfully—to pray daily—not just out of desperation for our children but because we desperately need to know the love of Jesus. There are many circumstances and conditions beyond our control, but with Jesus as our closest friend—*a real living person, not just an idea*—we will receive all we need to love our children well and help them make it safely Home.

---

[10] Joseph Langford, *Mother Teresa's Secret Fire* (Huntington, IN: Our Sunday Visitor, 2016), 297.

Chapter 6

HUSBANDS AND FATHERS

One cannot overstate the importance of the unique, irreplaceable role that fathers play in establishing, building, maintaining, and passing on the faith to their children. In this chapter, I, Peter, want to speak directly to husbands and fathers about the amazing vocation the Lord has given us, the authority He has placed in our hands, the obstacles men often face in fully embracing our vocation, and some practical tools to make sure we are laying the right foundation.

Many years ago, a priest friend gave a simple but brilliant talk on fatherhood that helped give me God's vision and a foundation for my role as a father. Stated simply, he said, "Fatherhood is God's idea, one that flows from God's own nature. Jesus revealed to us that God, the Creator of all things, is a father. And every man is called to participate in the fatherhood of God."

St. Paul said, "I bow my knees before the Father, from whom every family in heaven and on earth is named" (Eph 3:14–15). Ultimately, God is the Father of us all. Family is His idea, the one natural institution that He established and the foundational building block of every society and civilization. At its deepest level, family according to Scripture is the image of God. Together the husband and wife, in the unity and love they share, and the children that are born of that love, and the community they live together, is a living sign, an image of God.

Jesus came to reveal the Father and to restore us to right relationship with God, to forgive our sins, to lead us out of slavery, alienation, and all that separates us from God our Father. Through Baptism He transforms us, delivers us from our orphaned state, and gives us "power to become children of God" (John 1:12). Jesus unites, restores, and establishes us as sons of the Father through the indwelling presence of the Holy Spirit given to us in Baptism. It is the Holy Spirit within us who heals our hearts, enabling us to receive the love of the Father, to know Him, and to approach Him with confidence. As St. Paul expressed so beautifully in Romans 8:15:

> For you did not receive the spirit of slavery to fall back into fear, but you have received the spirit of sonship. When we cry, "Abba! Father!" it is the Spirit himself bearing witness to our spirit that we are children of God.

This work of God in us is the foundation and source of our identity, confidence, and power that enables us to live our vocation as fathers. We are sons, not orphans or slaves. Jesus has given us a share in His relationship and position with the Father. The Spirit and the Son reveal the Father; they teach us who He is and enable us to understand how we as men participate in the liberating mission of Jesus by being fathers. This is our primary vocation. Fatherhood is what we are made for; it is the completion of manhood. Like our Father in heaven, we participate in the generation of life, we exercise authority in love, we govern, protect, watch over, teach, inspire, and lead. Our children, who are eternal creatures, have been entrusted to our care. As fathers this is our most important life's work. Our key role is to lead our families to Christ and to raise them up in the Lord.

The spiritual vision of Christian family life is a high calling and a great adventure. It is the place where we most fundamentally live out our baptismal call as priests, prophets, and kings. We are priests who lead our families in the worship of God, prophets who pass on the faith through how we live and what we teach, and kings who govern as servant leaders of our families.

This vision of the family and of Christian manhood is under intense spiritual attack today. The centerpieces of today's culture wars are the redefinition of human identity, the deconstruction of the traditional family, and the rejection of who we are as male and female. The complementary roles and the God-given authority of parents are a bulwark against evil and a restraint against the powers of the world, the flesh, and the devil. The father is the family's first protector, guardian, and defender. That is why the devil fights to mock, neuter, and undermine authentic masculinity. He wants unfettered access to our children. The best way for him to reach that goal is to disarm men.

The good news is that the only way he can disarm us is if we simply put down our weapons. The devil has no power over a man who is living under the Lordship of Jesus. Jesus told the Apostles on Holy Thursday that the "ruler of this world [the devil] . . . has no power over me" (John 14:30). That means every man who is baptized into Christ can say the same thing: "the devil has no power over me!" Satan fears the man of faith who stands on this fundamental truth: "he who is in you is greater than he who is in the world" (1 John 4:4).

This authority is not based on a man's perfection or performance but on the presence and power of the Holy Spirit who dwells within him. Jesus has given us a share in His victory over the devil: "He disarmed the principalities and powers and made a public example of them, triumphing over them" (Col 2:15). Jesus has given that authority to weak and broken men like you and me. The devil seeks to steal that authority through deceptions and accusations, convincing men that their weaknesses and failures disqualify them before God. That's a lie! Don't believe him and don't dialogue with the devil. Instead, obey the word of God: "Humble yourselves therefore under the mighty hand of God, that in due time he may exalt you. Cast all your anxieties on him, for he cares about you. Be sober; be watchful. Your adversary the devil prowls around like a roaring lion seeking some one to devour. Resist him, firm in your faith" (1 Pet 5:6–9). The way forward is simple, but not easy. "Submit yourselves therefore to God. Resist the devil and he will flee from you" (Jas 4:7).

The Great Adventure

I characterize family life, and particularly the noble vocation of fatherhood, as the Great Adventure. Most men have a difficult time perceiving this. Instead, we pursue greatness through the achievement of high goals and heroic efforts outside the family—through sports, business, and military service and other things the world recognizes and rewards. When pursued in the right order, these can be genuinely good and even noble, but they are not the highest goods.

The following story may shed some light on this point. In the summer of 2010, our family had the great privilege of going to Israel with Debbie's Jewish family. On our return from Israel, we spent a weekend in Manhattan with our son Josh before dropping him off at West Point Military Academy. The first two nights, I woke up wide awake in the middle of the night due to jet lag. So, I walked the streets of the city that never sleeps from 3:00 a.m. to sunrise. People, taxis, lights, and open bars and restaurants were everywhere. Our last night in the city, I slept all night and dreamt that I was walking through Manhattan during rush hour with its unending activity and commotion. I loved the energy and the power of the city. As I stood in the middle of a busy, crowded street, the traffic stopped and all the people disappeared. I was alone in the city, not a soul in sight. At that moment in the silence, I heard a baby crying. I pursued the sound, and turning the corner, I saw a baby alone in the middle of the street on a blanket.

As I picked up the baby, I heard the Lord say to me, "Peter, look around you at the towering buildings, lights, and human effort that so captivates you. Now look into the eyes of this child. Do you see what I see? All that you see will pass away in the twinkling of an eye. Now, look at this baby—naked, powerless, and alone. This child will never pass away. I did not come to preserve the things man calls great. I came for this child and every person who bears the image of my Father. This child will live for eternity, either in Heaven or in Hell. This child, along with every human, is the real gold, the only thing of inestimable value on the earth. I came to seek and save not great cities, human power, or prestige. I came to save what is truly valuable, those who bear the image and likeness of my Father. Those who from all eternity are destined to live forever."

As Christian fathers and disciples of Jesus, we need to see and understand things with the mind of Christ. The Bible exhorts us: "Do not be conformed to this world but be transformed by the renewal of your mind, that you may prove what is the will of God, what is good and acceptable and perfect" (Rom 12:2). A renewed mind includes having the capacity to value things in their proper order and to then direct our time, talent, and treasure in the right proportion to the things that matter most. We cannot see the true measure of things without the help of the Holy Spirit, whom Jesus said, "will teach you all things, and bring to your remembrance all that I have said to you" (John 14:26).

Navigating the world's system of values and balancing its demands, priorities, and total commitment to its goals and rewards is not easy. It requires vigilance, discernment, courage, and a single-hearted determination to be *in the world* but *not of the world*. The key is to remain loyal to Jesus, which includes valuing what He most values and always making it our aim to please Him (2 Cor 5:9).

Without making the radical shift of putting Jesus and His will first and living and responding to the gravitational pull of Christ and His Kingdom, we will not be able to resist the powerful forces and the disordered energies of the world, the flesh, and the devil. St. Paul makes the choice before us clear:

> Now this I affirm and testify in the Lord, that you must no longer walk as the Gentiles walk, in the futility of their minds; they are darkened in their understanding, alienated from the life of

God because of the ignorance that is in them, due to their hardness of heart; . . . Put off the old man that belongs to your former manner of life and is corrupt with deceitful lusts, and be renewed in the spirit of your minds, and put on the new man, created after the likeness of God in true righteousness and holiness. (Eph 4:17–18, 22–24)

The "world" in this biblical sense is precisely that pattern of values and priorities—including the economic, political, social, and cultural forces—that resist the will of God. This world operates according to an entirely different calculus than God's when it comes to measuring what matters. This is a critical distinction every man needs to make to see things clearly. Without this biblical worldview settled deeply in a man's heart, he will end up living in twilight rather than entering fully into the light of Christ. Without that clear light, a man cannot see the true value of things, and as a result will remain subject to the futility of mind and darkness of understanding that St. Paul spoke about. He becomes "a double-minded man, unstable in all of his ways" (Jas 1:8). Tossed about and constantly torn between two poles, he lacks the clarity and conviction needed to make the sacrifices necessary to confidently and consistently lead his family under the Lordship of Jesus.

How is it possible for a man who is not a priest or a monk to live with this eternal perspective? To be motivated each day, all day, by a radically different set of values than the world in which he moves? He needs to find the treasure hidden in the field, to see and experience the superior pleasures of knowing Christ Jesus. Seeing and possessing this treasure provides the strength and motivation needed to resist the temptation to prioritize the goods of this world.

A humorous story told about St. Francis and Brother Bernard beautifully expresses this. After praying all night long in the woods near their monastery, Brother Bernard began shouting at the crack of dawn to his brothers as he re-entered the monastery, "Brothers! Brothers! There is no man anywhere, no matter how great, no matter how much he was promised in riches, who wouldn't happily carry a bag of dung to win this amazing treasure!"[1] In other words, if the richest, most powerful man, who is happily tied to this world and is the envy of all, discovered this treasure, he would gladly do anything to gain and keep it, even if it meant giving up everything and carrying a bag of manure through the city. He would be willing to pay any price, even to look like a fool. Brother Bernard understood that the radical sacrifice of living in total poverty that he and his brothers made would not be sustainable if not for Christ. But united to Christ and knowing they were doing His will, their daily burdens became a source of profound joy. In contemporary language, they knew they were "trading up" when they made that investment. In fact, they won the lottery!

Gaining the Treasure

The foundation of a man's spiritual leadership in the home is built on his relationship with Jesus. Everything flows from there, especially the kind of encouragement, confidence, and vision men need to see themselves as spiritual leaders and disciple-makers in their own homes.

---

[1] Brother Ugolino, *Little Flowers of St. Francis* (Brewter, MA: Paraclete Press, 2016), 40.

Unfortunately, few men have fathers who modeled spiritual leadership nor do they have the experience of being discipled by other men. As a result, men often hesitate to take up this challenge simply because they don't know what to do or where to start. They feel inadequate to the task and so they happily delegate spiritual leadership in the home to their wives.

There is a fundamental principle here: you cannot give away what you do not have. Christianity is a *new life* in Christ. It is not simply a set of dogmas, commandments, and moral principles, though it certainly includes these things. Spiritual leadership in the family is not just an exchange of information and the fulfillment of certain obligations; it's a matter of leading others—in this case, our wives and children—into a living, daily encounter with Jesus.

If you are living with Jesus each day—talking to Him, believing His promises, following His leadership—and seeking and receiving His grace through Scripture, sacraments, and prayer, you will be able to help others do the same. What flows into you will begin to flow out of you. Jesus promised, "I am the vine, you are the branches. He who abides in me, and I in him, he it is that bears much fruit, for apart from me you can do nothing" (John 15:5).

Faith alive in a man as an experience of power, and new life is like sap flowing from a vine to its branches. The man will bring that life into his home. This life creates an atmosphere of faith in the home; it is part of the air that is breathed and is gradually expressed in habits that communicate a living awareness that Jesus is with us. The way of life of the family takes shape around Jesus through prayer, meals, celebrations, spiritual conversations, hospitality, service, and play.

What began with a couple's individual commitments and experience of "abiding in the vine" becomes a shared experience in their marriage. Their union becomes life together with Christ, and from that source the entire family begins to receive Christ-life. Forming a family culture centered on Jesus is an organic process, one in which Jesus is fully engaged. If the abiding is there, the fruit will come from Jesus. It's not enough to simply check the boxes, to make sure the kids go to a Catholic school and attend Sunday school classes and youth groups. As important as these are, they have a primarily supportive function to reinforce an already-lived reality.

These are the important questions we must ask ourselves as fathers: "Who is Jesus to me? Have I invited Him to be the center and purpose of my life? Am I abiding in the vine?" As a young man, I began to answer those questions with clarity and purpose, relying on the promises of God. Now, with decades of experience as a father and almost a decade of experience as a grandfather, I am amazed at the Lord's faithfulness. I know from experience that His promises are true; they are the most solid rock on which a man can stand. And what amazes me the most is that He demonstrates His faithfulness through weak and broken people like me. Through all the ups and downs, hardships, challenges, personal failures, doubts, and spiritual battles, He fulfills His promises! That is good news!

Brothers, you can take this to the bank: if you seek Him first in your life, in your marriage, and in your family, He will lead you and give you the help you need to fulfill your vocation. As I mentioned above, we have an adversary, the devil, who works day and night to steal this promise. His greatest lie is that God is not faithful to His promises to you. He tries to disqualify you through accusation: "You're a failure, God has abandoned you, God is disappointed, frustrated, angry with you, your life will not end well, you might as well give up and give in." He does all he can to fill you with fear, anger, shame, hopelessness, and, ultimately, despair.

Brothers, our first task is simply to stand, to believe, to keep leaning into and trusting in the promises of God, one day at a time. The war has already been won; the devil has already been defeated. As a wise priest once told me, to live by faith is to lean on God with your whole life in such a way that if He wasn't there you would fall flat on your face.

God has appointed and equipped you as the father of your family. You can fulfill this assignment from the Lord, despite your obvious limitations, because it is His work. You can step into this vocation with a confidence built on expectant faith. He promised to be with you always, until He calls you Home. Lean into that promise by first deciding, if you haven't already done so, to enthrone Jesus in your heart as your Lord and Savior (1 Pet 3:15). Second, ask Him each day for the full release of the spiritual power He has bestowed upon you through the Holy Spirit in your Baptism, Confirmation, and Sacrament of Matrimony. Remember, Jesus is the Christ, which means anointed one. "God anointed Jesus of Nazareth with the Holy Spirit and with power" (Acts 10:38). He told the Apostles before He ascended into heaven to prepare themselves for what He was about to do:

> *You heard from me, for John baptized with water, but before many days you shall be baptized with the Holy Spirit. (Acts 1:4–5)*

> *. . . you shall receive power when the Holy Spirit has come upon you; and you shall be my witnesses in Jerusalem and in all Judea and Samaria and to the end of the earth. (Acts 1:8)*

Marriage, family, and fatherhood are all natural realities. But Christian marriage, family and fatherhood are realities taken to another level—they are born of the Holy Spirit. The Spirit gives us a new power and a new capacity to live an entirely new way of life. St. Paul calls us to examine our faith in this regard: "Examine yourselves, to see whether you are holding to your faith. . . . Do you not realize that Jesus Christ is in you?" (2 Cor 13:5). The One who "destroyed death and brought life and immortality," (2 Tim 1:10 NIV) He who disarmed the principalities and powers and made a public example of them triumphing over them through the Cross, dwells in you!

You have been given all you need to be the husband and father the Lord has destined you to be. He is giving you power to be His witness, to make Him known to your children and grandchildren through your words and deeds. It is a power strong enough to help you overcome all that holds you back—your fears, insecurities, laziness, habitual patterns of sin, brokenness you may have brought into marriage from your past, and the wounds and dysfunctions from your family of origin.

These two steps, living under the Lordship of Jesus and learning to "be led by the Spirit" (Gal 5:18) or to "walk by the Spirit" (Gal 5:25) are the foundations of fatherhood in Christ. Living with Jesus each day with the help, leading, counsel, encouragement, correction, and power of the Holy Spirit is the source from which new life, conversion, and the fruits of your vocation become a reality:

> You did not choose me, but I chose you and appointed you that you should go and bear fruit and that your fruit should abide. (John 15:16)

I've taken considerable space to underline these two foundation stones because they are often overlooked. For many, the spiritual gifts given through the sacraments lay dormant and undiscovered, and parents are ill-prepared for the challenge and high adventure of Christian family life.

It Takes Two

When a husband and wife are walking by faith and are alive in the Spirit, they have a precious gift. With Jesus at the center of a marriage, when the Holy Spirit is acknowledged and welcomed, the couple can attain a deep unity of heart and mind. They not only grow in deeper intimacy with one another, but they also share the growth in their spiritual union. Jesus said, "No longer do I call you servants . . . but I have called you friends, for all that I have heard from my Father I have made known to you" (John 15:15). The covenant promise that Jesus made in the Sacrament of Matrimony comes alive and flourishes, becoming a source of strength for the couple and the entire family. Their faith animates the life of the family and creates an atmosphere of living faith that becomes second nature. There is a shift from a lack of awareness of the value of these things and the drudgery of simply fulfilling obligations to a dynamic and enthusiastic way of life that defines and shapes the family's identity.

Each couple has their own unique struggles in trying to reach this kind of mutual sharing of life in Christ. It takes time. There will be obstacles to overcome, awkward moments, successes and failures, setbacks and advances. But over time, every obstacle can be overcome if you persevere in pursuing the Lord together.

Looking back, there were many times when it took work for Debbie and me to stay on the same page as we sought to build our family culture. One of the most important things we learned over time was how to handle our disagreements and how to, as St. Paul puts it, "maintain the unity of the Spirit in the bond of peace" (Eph 4:3). As a husband, I learned the importance of guarding Debbie's honor, despite how I may have felt in a particular moment. It is easy in the heat of an argument to say and do hurtful things. It is crucial as a husband and father that you always speak in a way that honors your wife and to never disrespect or humiliate her, especially in front of your children—and at the same time to never allow your children to speak or behave disrespectfully toward their mother. Right speech in the home is essential for establishing and maintaining a healthy family culture in the Lord. St. James gives a sober warning about the need to tame the tongue:

> So the tongue is a little member and boasts of great things. How great a forest is set ablaze by a small fire! The tongue is a fire. The tongue is an unrighteous world among our members, staining the whole body . . . no human being can tame the tongue—a restless evil, full of deadly poison. (Jas 3:5–6, 8)

In my experience, this is a place where fathers need to be vigilant and zealous to exercise authority when needed to maintain unity and peace. The right exercise of authority begins with modeling for your children what appropriate speech is but also being quick to take responsibility for personal failures. Children need to see that their parents practice what they preach. There were key moments in our marriage when I had to ask Debbie to forgive me for something I said in the heat of the moment. If my children heard it, I would repent to Debbie in their presence. Moments like this are humbling, but they are great learning opportunities. Parents must take the lead in helping their children understand and embrace the high ideal and expectations Jesus places before us. In little ways like this, we help our children understand what is of first importance to us.

Band of Brothers

Early in my life as a husband and father, I made an important decision based on the advice of other men that helped me tremendously. I sought out other men—brothers in Christ— who were pursuing the same goals I had for my marriage and family. Building a family culture requires Christian community. Every man needs support and friendships with other men who are rooted in Christ. For the past forty years, I've been part of different men's small groups where we share our lives, our victories and failures, and pray for one another. Most men carry their struggles, especially their failures, in isolation. Often living in denial, men are weighed down, sometimes tormented in crippling ways with fears, unresolved anger, sadness, and shame. They expend enormous amounts of emotional energy trying to put on a happy face—to look good. But behind the masks, many men are suffering under the weight of loneliness and self-condemnation.

Finally, do all you can to cultivate the virtue of zeal for the salvation of souls, beginning with your own, and for your spouse, children, and grandchildren. Resist the temptation to plateau. Beg the Holy Spirit to give you a deep, heartfelt awareness of what is at stake in this life and in the life to come. Seek to live with an eternal perspective and make eternal salvation the highest goal you desire for your children.

Chapter 7

WIVES AND MOTHERS

One of the most defining and enduring lessons in love came for me at a difficult time in my personal life as a young mother.

We had been married for almost four years and were settled in our domestic routine. Peter worked full-time in Catholic ministry, and I cared for our home, our two-and-a-half-year old daughter and our six-month-old son, helped out with youth ministry, and did some freelance writing. As I cleaned and cooked, did laundry and changed diapers, I struggled internally with this new phase of my life and the mostly hidden, mundane, tiring, and often thankless daily tasks.

I loved being a wife and mother and expressing my love in acts of service, but it was often difficult for me to believe that what I was doing really mattered and made a difference. Tired and lonely, I mistakenly wondered if a maid or a nanny (we couldn't afford either) could do all these tasks more efficiently and allow me more time to love and serve God. No matter how hard I tried or how much I prayed, I couldn't shake the nagging sense that these small daily acts of sacrificial love were not that important or valuable.

One day in early spring, Peter and I received an invitation to speak at a conference on the family in Germany. I was excited for the opportunity to travel and minister with Peter! With Michael in tow and Sarah with my parents, Peter and I departed for our five days abroad.

From the moment our plane took off, everything seemed to go wrong. Michael cried for much of the overseas flight, our luggage was lost and delivered to the hotel twelve hours later; my jewelry was stolen and jars of baby food were smashed between my nice clothes. All of this could have been endured were it not for the news we received from the organizers upon our arrival. They had overbooked presenters and there was only time in the conference schedule for one of us to speak. I was very disappointed, but as I listened to Peter's talk, followed by a standing ovation, I knew it was supposed to be him who presented at the conference. That night as I nursed my baby, I tearfully asked the Lord why He had brought me all the way to Germany to "do nothing."

The next day, we entered the large hall for the closing session. I had been so absorbed with my own situation that I hadn't even inquired about who was speaking. As we looked for our seats, a conference worker stopped me with a special request from the speaker. Mother Teresa of Calcutta wanted a few mothers with their babies to sit on the stage with her as she spoke. Of course I eagerly agreed, and when Peter asked me where I was going, I turned to him with a wry smile and said, "I'm going to sit with Mother Teresa!" The ten babies in arms on that stage were remarkably quiet as we all listened intently to this tiny nun in her blue and white sari and tattered sweater. She reminded us that the first one to greet Jesus was His cousin John in the womb, and that it is the obligation of society to protect the family and its most helpless members.

Only one thing could have surpassed my experience that morning. Before we knew it, the moms were directed to an area backstage where Mother Teresa stood to greet each one of us individually. As I waited nervously in line, my only thoughts were to keep Michael quiet and to be fully present in the moment. As I leaned down to greet her with my son in my arms, Mother Teresa traced the Sign of the Cross on his forehead and pressed a small silver Miraculous Medal in my palm. As I turned to go, she grasped me by the hand and pulled me close, with a gaze that forced me to look into her eyes. "You must never forget," she said, "your job as a mother is the *most important* job in the whole world!"

I walked away stunned. God had sent me across the ocean to answer the deeper questions of my heart, to hear a truth from this holy woman (who twenty-five years later would be canonized a saint), that I couldn't receive and believe at home. The impact of that fortuitous meeting with Mother Teresa didn't fade as I went home to my *"most important job* in the whole world." Her words that day not only affirmed my vocation, but as I read more about her life and explored her writings, I discovered a secret weapon. She was teaching me a powerful way to love that transformed both my vocation as a wife and mother and my ministry to women.

In those years of hiddenness, I was able to embrace her notion that to truly change the world I must go home and love my family. Over time, I learned to *do small things with great love*, to love the person right in front of me, to smile more often, make more time for prayer, and define success by small acts of faithful obedience.

There is a story about Elizabeth of the Trinity, who was hurrying to complete a task in the convent when one of the older sisters stopped her to ask what she was doing. "Oh, my mother," she answered, "I am loving."[1] Whatever that insignificant task was, it had been made invaluable by love. In my own life, this revelation of what it means to truly love and the transformational power of love has indelibly shaped my identity and my vocation. Everything we do, great or small, appreciated or hidden, is made infinite when it is infused with love for God and others.

Remember Who You Are

Of course there were days when I felt overwhelmed by fatigue or discouragement and it was difficult to remember these important truths. One Saturday morning during family chore time, I was reluctantly cleaning the toilet, unhappily amazed at my boys' tireless ability to miss their target. I may have been grumbling a bit, wishing my head was in a book and not in the toilet, when my daughter Sarah came excitedly into the bathroom with a bouquet of a dozen yellow roses. "Mom, these were just delivered, and I have no idea who they're from," she exclaimed. I pulled the card from the wrapping to reveal an unsigned message: "Thank you for all you do. God sees when no one else does." I assumed that Peter had sent the flowers, but when I questioned him, he thoroughly denied it, pointing out that he certainly would have taken the credit for such a thoughtful gesture. I never did solve the mystery, but the Lord used

---

[1] Claire Dwyer, *This Present Paradise* (Bedford, NH: Sophia Institute Press, 2020), 148.

it to patiently remind me again—like a small child that needs reassurance—that I was seen and valued. He was also leading me into a greater maturity that would enable me to confidently and peacefully live out my vocation in every season of my life—with or without flowers!

As women, our identity can often be tied up in the external standards of worldly success: what we do and accomplish, how we look and what we have, who we know, and even how our kids are doing. As women of faith, we must remember the profound truth articulated by St. Teresa Benedicta of the Cross: "The world doesn't simply need what women have, it needs what women are."[2] Our fundamental identity is not defined by *what* we do but by *who* we are as beloved daughters of God.

This identity is bestowed on us by God as a gift; it can never be earned and never lost. I often tell young girls that God loves them no matter what; there is nothing we can do to make Him love us more, and nothing we can do to make Him love us less. He loves us, period. This is perhaps one of the most difficult truths to believe.

Many women strive to get everything done and to be everything to everyone. And they are tired, fearful, anxious, lonely, and disappointed. They have this relentless, underlying anxiety that they are failing. Behind the daily juggling act of marriage, family, work, and volunteering can be the question: Will I ever be and do enough?

We can allow ourselves to be defined by our "doing" because we don't really know who we are apart from it. God wants to deliver us from the imprisoning sense that we should be someone other than who we are, that we

---

[2] Leah Darrow, *The Other Side of Beauty: Embracing God's Vision for Love and True Worth* (Nashville, TN: Thomas Nelson, 2017), 17.

must prove ourselves worthy of love and affection. In our insecurity and striving, Jesus tenderly speaks to us, "Come to me, all who labor and are heavy laden, and I will give you rest" (Matt 11:28). What we all long for is the freedom to know who we truly are and to rest and rejoice in our identity.

In an ideal world, our identity is shaped by our parents and family. But we live in a fallen, broken world full of imperfect people. In my own life, the powerful voice of shame has tried to rob me of my identity by telling me that I am defined by my sin, by what I have done and what has been done to me. Like Adam and Eve in the garden, we shamefully cover ourselves and hide from God's presence. We can only know who we are if we come out of hiding and we allow God to look at us, even in our brokenness. As St. Thérèse wrote in one of her poems, "I need the glance of my Divine Savior."[3] Jesus' glance is one of hope. He doesn't see our mistakes, sins, and human blemishes. He doesn't see the "not yet" or "almost" or "not quite enough." He sees His beloved daughter who radiates the glory and splendor she is created to reflect. Let the Lord look at you. At the end of our lives, each of us will stand alone before Him, and His love, approval, and acceptance will be the only thing that matters.

As wives, mothers, sisters, and daughters we bring unique qualities, described by Pope St. John Paul II as the feminine genius, into the heart of our families and all of society, making an indispensable contribution to the growth of a culture.[4] We must each allow the Lord

---

[3] St. Therese of Lisieux, *The Poetry of Saint Therese of Lisieux* (Washington, DC: ICS Publications, 1996).

[4] Pope St. John Paul II, *Letter to Women* (June 29, 1995).

to reveal to us the distinctive way He is calling us to love Him and express the gift of our womanhood to those around us.

A few years ago in prayer, I sensed the Lord telling me, "You will never be Mother Teresa." As you can imagine, I was greatly discouraged and confused. But then I realized the truth that God was trying to impress upon me. I will never be Mother Teresa, but as Debbie Herbeck I can love God as no one else has loved Him. So why would I want to be a second- or third-rate version of someone else when I can be a first rate, unique version of myself? St. Catherine of Siena said, "Be who you are created to be and you will set the world on fire." What matters most in life is not *what you do*, but *who you are*. Define yourself as a daughter who is radically loved by her Father. Define your value by what you are worth to God—because you are someone who is worth dying for.

Authentic Community

Despite the busyness of life, many mothers experience isolation and loneliness, especially when their children are younger. Peter traveled internationally when our children were small and our extended family lived out of state. I remember one afternoon, standing at the living room window with a baby in my arms and a toddler underfoot, watching Peter's car pull away and feeling utterly alone. Intellectually, I knew that the same God who was going with Peter to the airport was also staying home with me. But in those challenging days, I needed a "God with skin on." No matter how strong and competent we are, we are not meant to walk this path alone but to live in communion with one another. Our marriages and family are the primary way that we image the strongest community, the Holy Trinity. But we also need strong, authentic, supportive relationships with other women whose source is Christ's love. Henri Nouwen describes community as "a fellowship of little people who together make God visible in the world."[5] The goal isn't to close ranks and withdraw safely into our little group of like-minded people. It is to point to a greater, larger love, to become a window through which others can get a glimpse of the unseen, infinite love of God.

It takes effort to cultivate authentic relationships. Podcasts, apps, online communities, and conferences are helpful and important, and sometimes our only option, but we also need real, face-to-face, in-person relationships with other strong Christian women. I have a group of close female friends and although we are scattered throughout the U.S. and Canada, whenever we talk on the phone or take our annual lake retreat together, we instantly reconnect. We freely share our joys and victories, the difficult situations we are facing, and we pray for one another. We all need honest conversations and accountability with other women who can speak to us with encouragement and motivation and fight for us when we are weary and say to us, "This is not God's best for you! Not today, Satan!"

But exhort one another every day, as long as it is called "today," that none of you may be hardened by the deceitfulness of sin. (Heb 3:13)

---

[5] Henri Nouwen, *The Essential Henri Nouwen* (Berkeley, CA: Shambhala Publications, 2009), 143.

Let the word of Christ dwell among you richly, as you teach and admonish one another with all wisdom, and as you sing psalms and hymns and spiritual songs with thankfulness in your hearts to God. (Col 3:16)

Through different seasons of my life, I have been part of a women's small group. It's often easy in these contexts to just stay on the surface and keep conversations centered around meal planning, schedules, sleep training, kids' activities, and at times even gossip and venting. To have authentic, supportive relationships we must be willing to go deeper, not just on issues but in matters of the heart, in our struggles and difficulties. These friendships should also be a place to rejoice together! It is often easier to complain than it is to live in gratitude; one produces despair and the other hope.

A significant pitfall for women can be the tendency toward comparison and competition. It is easy to view other women's lives through rose-colored glasses and wish our circumstances were different. This leads to loneliness, isolation, envy, and jealousy. We are called to community, not comparison, and to champion and not compete with one another. This means that we are not threatened or diminished by the way another woman expresses her vocation and uses her gifts and talents. In fact, the ability to rejoice in others' success means I am learning how to express the authentic love that St. Paul described:

> Love is gentle and consistently kind to all. It refuses to be jealous when blessing comes to someone else. . . . Love does not traffic in shame and disrespect, nor selfishly seek its own honor. Love is not easily irritated or quick to take

offense. Love joyfully celebrates honesty and finds no delight in what is wrong. Love is a safe place of shelter, for it never stops believing the best for others. (1 Cor 13:4–7 TPT)

When we as women are living with a spirit of generosity and gratitude, collaborating and supporting one another—in a neighborhood, school, organization, business, family, parish, or ministry—we are a force for tremendous good, working together toward the common goal of heaven. I believe that one of the most important aspects of my work with Be Love Revolution is to teach girls and young women how to grow authentic friendships and sisterhood in Christ so they can learn to love themselves and others in freedom and joy, confident in their identity as beloved daughters of the Father.[6]

Many of us have fallen prey to the devil's strategy of using personal wounds, disappointments, and miscommunication to create division. We must guard our minds, hearts, and mouths from negativity, criticism, and blame, and always choose to trust others' hearts, even if their actions aren't always what we want. This doesn't mean we condone, excuse, or ignore wrong behavior, but it helps us be aware of our true enemy. We can mirror God's mercy and unconditional love by not letting our emotions decide when or if we are going to offer or receive forgiveness. Practice forgiveness quickly so resentments don't form and remind yourself of the truth that God loves the other person as much as He loves you.

We can be assured that following Jesus, having a holy and healthy marriage, and raising faith-filled children

---

[6] For more, see the Be Love Revolution website at www.beloverevolution.com.

is going to be increasingly difficult in the days ahead. Scripture reminds us not to be surprised at the fiery ordeal, that the world hates us, or that we are misunderstood, marginalized, excluded, and even cancelled.[7] As the world grows darker, we cannot live in isolation from one another. We need strength, support, and encouragement from others. We need continual reminders about our true identity as God's daughters and why He is worth our sacrifices and sufferings. At each phase of life, it is important to find wise mentors and elder women who have known Jesus longer and have walked where you are trying to walk.

The Mother of All Mothers

As women entrusted with the gift of motherhood, we are called to make a sincere gift of self by giving ourselves away in a love that is total, complete, and fruitful. There is no better model or icon of motherhood than Mary, our Mother. Venerable Archbishop Fulton Sheen wrote, "If fatherhood has its prototype in the Heavenly Father, Who is the giver of all gifts, then certainly such a beautiful thing as motherhood shall not be without some original Mother, whose traits of loveliness every mother copies in varying degrees."[8] That original mother is Mary, the Mother of God. "She existed in the Divine Mind as an Eternal Thought before there were any mothers. She is the Mother of mothers."[9]

When Peter and I were dating, I began what I considered to be an intellectual exploration of the Catholic

---

[7] See 1 Peter 4:12; John 15:18–20; 2 Timothy 3:12; Luke 6:22; 1 John 3:13.
[8] Fulton Sheen, *The World's First Love* (San Francisco: Ignatius Press, 2010), 185.
[9] Sheen, *The World's First Love*, 13.

faith. Weekly meetings with a priest, daily study, and Mass attendance all helped me learn about the teachings and practices of the Church, but what I did not anticipate was the personal and maternal love and care that I received from Mary as she accompanied me on this journey.

My own mother did not have a significant role in my life during this important time, and in a simple yet profound way, as she had done with her cousin Elizabeth, Mary came to be with me in my time of need. Several months later, I knew that Christ was inviting me into His Body, the Church. It was Mary, the supreme Jewish Mother, who welcomed me home and became for me a shelter in which my soul could unfold.[10]

Throughout my years as a wife and mother, Mary's fiat has taught me that receptivity is the most fundamental act of both my human and spiritual life. As I've struggled with striving and self-reliance, Mary's humility and lowliness reminds me that my life is not so much about doing; rather, it is about welcoming through faith the immense gift offered freely to me by God. As my children were growing and becoming more independent, I related to Mary's anxious concern about leaving her Son behind in the Temple. Her example and maternal help have enabled me to entrust each one of my children (and now grandchildren) to the Father's plan, even when they were not where I wanted them to be. Mary's compassionate, maternal heart is so beautifully expressed at the wedding in Cana, when she is the first to notice that the wine has run out. Rather than taking the situation into her own hands, as we women tend to do, she brings the need to her Son with great faith in His supernatural

---

[10] Edith Stein, *Essays on Women* (Washington, DC: ICS Publications, 2017), 132.

power. "Do whatever He tells you" is the last time we hear her speak, and her clear yet deferential words invite us to deeper trust, faithfulness, and obedience to Jesus.

Mary, Mother of God, Mother of the Apostles, Mother of the Church never preached, promoted, or set up her ministry. For more than thirty years she never went far from her home, and she was content to live a hidden life of sacrificial love and faith. As women we all share in Mary's vocation—to welcome the life of God into our homes, families, and friendships through our daily yes to Him.

When the infant Jesus was presented in the Temple on the eighth day, Simeon prophesied that a sword would pierce her heart. As Mary stood at the foot of the Cross, she participated in the suffering of her Son with courageous faith and love. Whenever we are at the foot of the Cross, facing death, illness, fear, discouragement, loneliness, and darkness, Mary is there with us in our time of need, helping us unite our pain to her Son's suffering. Finally, we see Mary present in the Upper Room at Pentecost. The Holy Spirit, who overshadowed her in the beginning, now comes and dwells in the whole Church and births the Body of Christ. Like Mary, we are called to receive the life of the Spirit in a fuller way, to bear witness to the life of Christ to those around us through the power and presence of the Holy Spirit within us.

> It can thus be said that women, by looking to Mary, find in her the secret of living their femininity with dignity and of achieving their own true advancement. In the light of Mary, the Church sees in the face of women the reflection of a beauty which mirrors the loftiest sentiments of which the human heart is capable: the

self-offering totality of love; the strength that is capable of bearing the greatest sorrows; limitless fidelity and tireless devotion to work; the ability to combine penetrating intuition with words of support and encouragement.[11]

A Word to the Weary

It's not uncommon for many couples to come into their marriage in very different places in their spiritual life. Oftentimes when Peter and I give talks on marriage, women will say to me afterwards, "Your husband speaks with such conviction about his faith! I wish my husband was the active spiritual leader of our family. I don't think it's ever going to change." While it is difficult for either spouse when couples are not united in faith, we are called to persevere in prayer and love, trusting in God's plan and His patient and merciful love.

Elisabeth Leseur is a heroic example of holiness lived in the context of marriage and secular society. Her husband Felix was an adamant atheist who often opposed and ridiculed Elizabeth for her faith. She suffered much but her example, as well as her prayers and sacrifices, ultimately led to the conversion of her husband. She wrote in her diary: "My God, one day . . . soon . . . You will give me the immense joy of a full spiritual communion with my beloved husband—the same faith, and a life for both him and me that may be directed toward You!"[12] From then on, praying for her husband's conversion became the focus of her entire life.

---

[11] Pope St. John Paul II, Encyclical Letter on the Blessed Virgin Mary in the life of the Pilgrim Church *Redemptoris Mater* (March 25, 1987), § 46.

[12] Elisabeth Leseur, *The Secret Diary of Elisabeth Leseur* (Manchester, NH: Sophia Institute Press, 2002).

Elisabeth died at the age of forty-eight, after a seven-year battle with cancer. In a note that Elisabeth had written to Felix in the year of her death were the following words: "In 1905 I begged Almighty God to send me sufferings with which to pay the price of your soul. There is no greater love to be found in a woman than when she gives her life for her husband."[13]

Her death began his slow journey back to the Catholic faith. Felix Leseur later wrote, "From her journal I was able to perceive with clarity the interior significance of the life of Elisabeth, so great in her humility. I came to appreciate the splendor of that faith of which I had seen such marvelous effects. The eyes of my soul were opened, and I turned toward the God who called me. I confessed my sins to a priest and was reconciled with the Church." Three years after his wife's death, Felix returned to the Church and in 1919 he became a Dominican friar, and in 1923 he was ordained a priest.

I want to encourage all who are struggling in their marriages, who long for deeper spiritual conversion and communion with their spouse, not to give up hope but to continue to pray and fight for your marriage. Elisabeth Leseur's prayers and sacrifices for her husband arose out of a deep love for him, a desire for his eternal salvation, and trust in the Lord's merciful love. Ask the Lord to deepen your love for your husband, and to help you see what He sees and love what He loves in him.

---

[13] H.M. Magazine; *Elisabeth Leseur*, March 2, 2021

Chapter 8

BUILDING A LEGACY OF LOVE

There is a Hebrew phrase—*L'dor v'dor* which is translated: *from generation to generation*. It is understood to mean the transmission of Jewish values, rituals, traditions, history, and spiritual knowledge from one generation to the next. Within the Body of Christ, parents have the primary role to educate and evangelize their children with the goal of actively passing on to the next generation a faith and love for Jesus that is vibrant, fruitful, and holy.

Often when parents are in the midst of the childrearing years—stretched, challenged, and exhausted—it can be difficult to think beyond the week, let alone have a long-term strategic plan for raising up the next generation of saints. Just as Rome wasn't built in a day, the building of a strong Catholic family through which love of God and neighbor is transmitted takes time (weeks, months, and years!), patience, perseverance, and trust that God is infinitely more invested in our children's lives than even we are as their parents. Even when children are grown and making choices that are often contrary to what we think is best for them, God, their loving Father, is still actively pursuing them and waiting patiently for their return.

Today our four children are faith-filled, Catholic young adults, and some are married and raising their own families now. Although our daily, hands-on parenting responsibilities have changed, we realize that our job isn't quite finished. As parents, grandparents, and mentors to young people, we see the importance of building a legacy of love and faith that is actively passed on to the next generation and beyond.

For the past thirty-seven years I, Debbie, have had the privilege of directing Pine Hills, a weeklong summer camp whose aim is to help junior-high-aged girls encounter the love of Christ. My own daughters, daughters-in-law, and nieces have attended and served on staff at camp. When Audrey, our first grandchild, was three, she joined her mom on staff, and that week of camp has become the highlight of her summer for the past six years. When she was four years old, we walked through camp together and suddenly she stopped and exclaimed, "Grandma, I know why you made this camp! You made it for ME! I can't wait to bring my friends and cousins and to be a counselor one day. I want everyone to know about camp and about Jesus!" Her precious insight articulated for me the supreme value and beauty of building and passing on a legacy of faith and love to our children and grandchildren.

As grandparents, we try to practically support our adult children in their role as parents. Although our schedules are still quite full, we make it a priority to spend weekly time with our young grandkids and to develop personal and individual relationships with each one of them. It is such a joy when our own kids send their young children to us for answers to their budding theological questions like: "Grandpa, what happened to all those people who died before Jesus rose from the dead? Grandma, is the devil real?"

We schedule regular family dinners or brunches that begin with prayer and family vacations that include Mass, Bible stories, Scripture memorization, and night prayer. Our youngest daughter still brings friends over for dinner, spiritual conversation, and prayer, and all of them now extend the hospitality they learned as children by opening their own homes to others.

We give our adult children and grandkids spiritual books, devotionals, good podcasts, talks, and other resources to help them grow spiritually. We try not to impose on them our opinions or views about how they are leading their own families but gladly offer advice and practical wisdom when we are asked. Overall, we have found that the best practice is to be present to our adult children in their joys and sorrows, be available to help in practical ways, and pray for them daily, asking the Holy Spirit how we can best love each of them. Watching our adult children grow in faith, wrestle with the unique challenges of the times, serve the Lord and proclaim the Gospel, choose wonderful spouses, and raise their young families to know Christ has brought us great joy and a renewed commitment to help the next generations say as we did, "As for me and my house, we will serve the Lord" (Josh 24:15).

Here is a powerful prayer from Ephesians 3:14–19 that we can pray for our families and the generations to come:

> For this reason I kneel before the Father, from whom every family in heaven and on earth derives its name. I pray that out of his glorious riches he may strengthen you with power through

his Spirit in your inner being, so that Christ may dwell in your hearts through faith. And I pray that you, being rooted and established in love, may have power, together with all the Lord's holy people, to grasp how wide and long and high and deep is the love of Christ, and to know this love that surpasses knowledge—that you may be filled to the measure of all the fullness of God. Now to him who is able to do immeasurably more than all we ask or imagine, according to his power that is at work within us, to him be glory in the Church and in Christ Jesus throughout all generations, for ever and ever! Amen. (NIV)

Chapter 9

ALL THINGS ARE POSSIBLE

The recent statistics that point to the decline in faith among Catholics, and among the young in particular, can be alarming. Many Catholic parents experience the pain of watching their young adult children leave the Church, not marry in the Church, and not baptize or raise their children in the faith. Saddened and discouraged, many parents (and grandparents) don't know where to turn for help.

Over the years, when I, Peter, have been discouraged or worried about my children's faith lives, I think about my mother. She was the spiritual anchor in our home. She reminded me of the persistent widow in the Bible who wouldn't stop interceding on behalf of her loved ones (Luke 18:1–8). Despite the many opportunities to be discouraged about the faith of her seven children, she chose to keep her eyes on the Lord. Daily prayer that included the Rosary, Scripture reading, and intercession was a lifeline for her, and, without question, it was the means by which all seven of her children, including some of us who drifted far for a time, came back to the faith.

My mother's decision to daily choose faith, hope, and love, to put her troubles in the hands of Our Lord and Our Lady, and to keep her eyes set on Jesus is a source of genuine inspiration to me and my siblings. It's important to remember every day that we are not alone, that the Lord is with us, He hears our prayers, and we can trust in Him. He loves our children and grandchildren more than we do, and He is fighting for their salvation day and night.

Discouragement is one of the devil's most potent weapons. He knows the only way he can defeat us is if we give in to discouragement and lay down our weapons. Our fundamental posture in this battle as parents, grandparents, and disciples is always the same: We are called to stand on the rock that is Christ (Eph 6:13). We must keep our eyes on Him, put all our trust in His promises, and follow His leadership. He will do the rest. Although, humanly speaking, situations can seem impossible, Jesus assures us that with God all things are possible (Matt 19:26).

The Underrated Power of Parents

There is some encouraging news about faith and family that comes from a large study led by Christian Smith, Professor of Sociology and Director of the Center for the Study of Religion and Society at the University of Notre Dame. In 2020, he gave the annual Yale Divinity School Ensign Lecture, entitled: "Parents, the REAL Pastors: The Absolute Centrality of Parenting in Passing on Religious Faith and Practice to the Next Generation."[1]

---

[1] See Christian Smith, "Parents, the REAL Pastors: The Absolute Centrality of Parenting in Passing on Religious Faith and Practice to the Next Generation," May 18, 2020, https://www.youtube.com/watch?v=i9TPqSf5ab0/.

His presentation focused on the third stage of one of the largest longitudinal studies of the religious lives of young people in America. The study tracked the lives of three thousand young people between the ages of thirteen and seventeen over a fifteen-year period. Smith summarized the findings this way: "No other conceivable causal influence–including clergy, youth pastors, youth group programs, missions/service trips, religious schools, religious peers, etc., comes remotely close to matching the influence of parents on the religious faith and practices of youth. . . . Parents dominate, wipe out all other effects, no way to change it in any other statistical model, it is just huge."[2]

This is encouraging news! Despite what so many experts have told us for decades, parents are relevant. Not only are parents important in the formation and ultimate choices their children make in matters of faith, nothing else comes close to their impact.

What we found especially encouraging is the actual data related to what most impacted the young people who made it through their teen years into the age of emerging adults (twenty-eight to thirty-two) with a living faith—one which, like that of their parents, is shaping their personal and family lives. The study found three key practices or habits of life the parents of these emerging adults shared in common.

The first was the importance faith played in the lives of both parents. Mom and Dad personally embraced and lived their faith. That embrace included weekly church attendance for the family. Second, the family, not just the parents, engaged in religious activities outside of weekly church services such as mission trips, serving

---

[2] Smith, "Parents, the REAL Pastors."

soup kitchens, etc. The third, and most impactful, practice was that the family—both parents—talked about religious topics in the normal course of life. Essentially, these families engaged together in age-specific spiritual conversations in which questions were regularly raised and openly addressed.

There is additional helpful data in this study, but for us these three practices, which were the big takeaways from the study itself, were very encouraging because they are all very doable! You don't have to be a theologian, a pastor, or an adolescent psychologist to effectively pass on the faith to your children. As Smith put it, these parents are the "real pastors" of their children. Other ministries directed to youth in the Church such as religious schools, youth outreaches, good pastors, and mentoring programs make important contributions, but their work is supplemental. That shouldn't surprise us, as Church documents on family life often underline that parents are the first teachers and primary disciplers of the next generation.

Unfortunately, the wider culture, and even some voices in the Church, make it seem like the raising of children, especially once they reach adolescence, should be left to the "experts" both inside and outside the Church. That attitude has undermined the confidence of parents and has led, in many cases, to the abdication of their unique authority and responsibility.

In some ways this study confirms what we, along with many other families in our parish, have tried to do in raising our own children. In its simplest form, the key is to build a culture—family habits, practices, traditions, conversations—and a kind of atmosphere centered on the person of Jesus in the life of the Church. This way of life, led by the parents, flows quite naturally from their own individual and shared faith as a couple. As they seek to live with Jesus, to love and follow His leadership in their own lives, that love shapes the family culture, making it a domestic Church and a dwelling place of God in the Spirit. This study should encourage us all to press on with confidence as we seek to pass on the faith to our children.

The call to remain faithful, to persevere to the end, is a consistent theme throughout the Scriptures, and this rings especially true in the area of marriage and family, where the spiritual battle has intensified. *Don't give up! Fight for your marriage!* Some or most of us may never seriously contemplate divorce, but we can give up in small, daily ways by failing to always choose love. We can allow annoyances, disappointments, and hurts to turn into resentment, mistrust, and indifference.

We cannot overstate the importance of praying for your spouse. Ask God to deepen your love for your spouse, to help you to see what He sees and love what He loves. God wants to help our marital love mature into a deepening trust, devotion, and commitment that is often forged by trials, illness, suffering, weakness, and humility. Our mission as parents is a marathon, not a sprint, and we must not grow weary or give up the fight, even when our children seem resistant or indifferent to the Gospel. In this extraordinary and challenging time in the history of the world and the Church, Jesus wants to raise up warriors and saints. Let us entrust our spouses, children, and grandchildren to Him and truly believe that *"with God all things are possible"* (Matt 19:26; Mark 10:27).

Open Wide the Doors

The words of St. John Paul II have been for us a great source of inspiration and consolation over the years as we've sought to build a family culture centered on the Lord. As he stepped onto the balcony of St. Peter's Basilica after just being elected successor to the Chair of St. Peter, he exclaimed: "Be not afraid . . . open wide the doors to Christ!"[3]

That simple exhortation expresses the first step and guiding principle for every couple who seeks to make their home a dwelling place of God in the Holy Spirit. It provides the attitude of heart, posture, hope and expectation, and confidence needed to strike out on the great adventure the Lord has set before us.

The words of St. John Paul II had great power in part because they flowed from his own experience, which began in his own family. Despite the many tragedies and sorrows—living through the Nazi and Communist occupations in Poland and the deaths of his mother when he was just eight years old, his older brother when he was twelve, and his father when he was twenty, he lived with great hope and confidence in God. He drew strength from his parents, especially his father, who taught him how to pray and how to have a relationship with the Holy Spirit.

St. John Paul II grew and was nourished by the noble, living faith of his mother and father and their profound trust in the promises of God. They brought him into their friendship and devotion to Our Lord, Our Lady, the Holy Spirit, and the saints. He became the great "witness to hope" because he grew up in an

---

[3] John Paul II, Homily of His Holiness John Paul II for the Inauguration of His Pontificate, St. Peter's Square (October 22, 1978).

environment of hope in a place and a time that seemed devoid of all reason to hope.

The Lord wants our marriages and families to be witnesses to hope! How can we overcome our own inadequacies and failures, fear of the unknown, the power of the world, and the devil's strategies against us? Open wide the doors to Christ! Open the door of your heart, let Him in, all the way in, every day! Open the door of your marriage, invite Him to be at the center of your relationship. Teach your children to do the same; help them know what it means to invite Jesus into their hearts and what it means to live daily with Him.

The psalmist reminds us that "unless the Lord builds the house, those who build it labor in vain" (Ps 127:1). We don't need to be afraid to begin building because we lack a full set of blueprints, a complete toolbox, training, or experience. The Lord is the builder! He knows that He has called us to break ground for a project we don't have the capacity to accomplish on our own. His great joy is to work with us and in us to create a beautiful, entirely unique marriage and family that our Father in heaven has prepared for us from all eternity!

In his inspiring encyclical on hope, *Spe Salvi*, Pope Benedict XVI wrote, "the one who hopes lives differently."[4] Hope produces confidence—a virtue given by the Holy Spirit that enables us to have deep confidence that the promises of God are true and unshakable.

By His grace, over time our trust in Him will deepen and the weight of fear, worry, and anxiety about the past, present, or future will gradually decrease. If we stay with Jesus and entrust ourselves to His faithfulness, we will be

---

[4] Pope Benedict XVI, Encyclical Letter on Christian Hope *Spe Salve* (November 30, 2007), § 2.

less troubled by the troubles of life and the fruits of the Holy Spirit will begin to emerge—including an abiding joy and peace.

As we all endeavor to faithfully live out our vocation of marriage and family life, let us remember our ultimate goal is heaven—to live in the school of love so that one day we can live in love with God forever. This is our joy and our hope, and so we are filled with gratitude. Let us rejoice and like the psalmist exclaim: "O taste and see that the Lord is good" (Ps 34:8).

REFLECTION AND DISCUSSION QUESTIONS FOR PERSONAL OR GROUP USE

Introduction

Peter and Debbie share their stories of conversion and a deepening life of faith.

For Personal Prayer

Take time individually to think about your own story and try to answer these questions: What parts of your story, including your family of origin and my past, have left you wounded and in need of deeper healing? Who is Jesus to me? Have you invited Him to be the center and purpose of your life?

Reflection and Discussion Questions

What practical steps might you take to grow in your own relationship with Jesus and make Him the center of your life?

_____
_____
_____
_____
_____
_____
_____

Couples' Reflection and Discussion

Develop and discuss some individual goals for deepening your faith life and living as disciples.

_____
_____
_____
_____
_____
_____
_____
_____

Reflection and Discussion Questions

Set aside time together with your spouse to share your personal stories with one another.

Together with Christ

Communication is key! With so much going on in family life, communication can be lacking not only regarding practical matters but also in the areas of unspoken expectations and unmet emotional needs. Pray together for the grace to be honest and open about your wants, needs, desires, and for the ability to prioritize ongoing growth in communication as a couple.

Chapter 1: Welcome to the Battle

Today, God's plan for marriage and family is at the center of an intense spiritual battle. An important first step in building a strong marriage and family culture is to perceive the spiritual context in which we live and to understand the forces that are set against us.

For Personal Prayer

Take time individually to identify the areas in your marriage and family life where you have not been vigilant and proactive against the world, the flesh, and the devil. Share your insights with your spouse.

_____

_____

_____

_____

_____

_____

_____

Reflection and Discussion Questions

What practical ways can you "put on the whole armor of God, that you may be able to stand against the wiles of the devil" (Eph 6:11)?

_____
_____
_____
_____
_____
_____
_____
_____

Couples' Reflection and Discussion

Discuss together the ways you see this spiritual battle being played out in the current culture and how it might be affecting your marriage and family life.

_____
_____
_____
_____
_____
_____
_____
_____

Reflection and Discussion Questions

God promises to give us all the grace we need to win the battle! How can you dispose yourselves and your children to more fully receive His grace?

_____

_____

_____

_____

_____

_____

_____

Together with Christ

Media and technology have provided the greatest challenge to parenting in the last decade, with a rapid acceleration in the past five years. There may be no way to turn back the clock, but we can help our children (and ourselves) to have greater detachment and freedom from its effects. Pray together for God's wisdom on this topic. Then, write down a list of family rules to help formalize your approach to media and technology. (For example: no cellphones or television during mealtimes, no cellphones or laptops in bedrooms, and age-appropriate screen time limits.)

Chapter 2: Three Is Not a Crowd!

Unless the Lord builds the house, its laborers (no matter how hard we work!) labor in vain. It is essential as we build a life together to begin with the right foundation, to actively and intentionally put our marriage and family under the Lordship of Jesus. This means practically implementing a way of life that keeps God at the center and expresses our trust in Him.

For Personal Prayer

During courtship and early marriage, what expectations did you have about marriage and one another that were unrealistic?

_____
_____
_____
_____
_____
_____
_____

Reflection and Discussion Questions

What practical habits and rituals might you implement in your marriage and family life to center God in everything and express deeper trust in His plan?

Couples' Reflection and Discussion

Pray together about a family motto you could adopt to help guide your particular family identity.

Reflection and Discussion Questions

What are some of your "do's" and "don'ts" for handling conflicts within your marriage and family?

_____
_____
_____
_____
_____
_____
_____
_____

Together with Christ

Finances can very easily become a source of stress and anxiety within marriage and family, and difficult economic circumstances can affect decisions about employment, mortgages, family planning, tithing, and schooling. If you don't already do so regularly, set aside an evening to go over the family budget and discuss long-term finances. Spend time talking about both short- and long-term financial issues and what goals you can commit to together. And then make sure that you follow up and regularly check in on your goals.

Chapter 3: The School of Love

When we place Christ at the center of our marriage and family all things are possible! Christian marriage is the school of love where, despite the limits of our own love, we can discover Christ's presence and power to teach us to love one another with the love that never fails. Christian marriage and family life are rooted in the self-donating love between a husband and wife who are seeking to imitate Jesus' love.

For Personal Prayer

What are some ways you have defined yourself and your vocation by *what you do* rather than by *who you are* and what you are made for?

_____

_____

_____

_____

_____

Reflection and Discussion Questions

How have your ideas about love been influenced by past experiences or the messages of the world around you? In what ways do those ideas differ from the Christian concept of love?

Couples' Reflection and Discussion

Take time to prayerfully read and reflect on St. Paul's instructions for husbands and wives in Ephesians 5:21–33. How are each of you living out this call in your marriage? In what ways do you need to grow?

Reflection and Discussion Questions

Are there any areas of unforgiveness toward your spouse or your children that need to be taken before the Lord? If so, ask Him for the grace to seek forgiveness and healing in those relationships.

_____

_____

_____

_____

_____

_____

_____

Together with Christ

The busyness and distractions of life can cause us to lose sight of what is most important, to be more functional than personal, and to lose the joy of building a life together with the ones we love. Make it your focus this week to prioritize personal connection even in the midst of everyday life. At family mealtimes, challenge yourself to be fully present to your family—to listen to their stories intently, to delight in their presence, and to savor the time you have together before getting back to work or chores.

Chapter 4: Building Our Way of Life

Christian family life is not simply a human construct that is the result of effort alone. Christian family life is a supernatural reality, lived in and through Christ. It is natural in every way—ordinary, messy, and hard, but it is also animated by the presence and power of the Holy Spirit.

For Personal Prayer

How can you set aside some time each day for personal prayer and what teamwork is required to support one another in this important endeavor?

_____
_____
_____
_____
_____
_____
_____

Reflection and Discussion Questions

What are some of the non-negotiable, important building blocks of your family life that reflect your and your spouse's mutual commitment to building a life centered on Christ?

_____

_____

_____

_____

_____

_____

Couples' Reflection and Discussion

Reflect together on the ways your family celebrates life together. What meaningful traditions and practices would you like to integrate into your family life?

_____

_____

_____

_____

_____

_____

If you don't already do this, schedule a weekly husband and wife meeting to discuss, assess, plan, and pray for the needs of your family.

_____

_____

_____

_____

_____

_____

_____

Together with Christ

Lack of parental unity is easy for kids to sniff out, especially as they get older and wiser. We didn't always agree on every decision we made, but we tried to never discuss or argue about it in front of the kids. When our kids came to one of us for a different outcome, we would always try to support the decision that had already been made. Talk about the aspects of your life together where you have different preferences, opinions, strengths. How might God be calling each of you to use your natural abilities and gifts to cultivate a strong and unified family?

Chapter 5: Mission Possible: Helping Our Children Encounter Christ

The Church exists to evangelize—an aspect of her fundamental identity and mission is to make disciples. Every household, the domestic Church, has a mission and a responsibility to make disciples and lead souls to heaven. If we do not intentionally and actively help our kids know and love Jesus personally, the secular world with its radicalized relativism and individualism will eagerly take our place as the loudest and most influential voice in their lives.

For Personal Prayer

Make a list of your hopes and desires for your children (or future ones). In what ways do worldly goals and success for them take precedence over God's ultimate goal for them?

_____

_____

_____

_____

Reflection and Discussion Questions

_____
_____
_____

Prayerfully and honestly consider ways in which you may not be creating a Christ-centered environment in your home or setting a good example for your spouse and children. What is one thing you can change to live more consistently and joyfully according to Gospel values?

_____
_____
_____
_____
_____
_____

Couples' Reflection and Discussion

In what ways are you teaching the faith to your children? What are some of your fears and inhibitions in doing so?

_____
_____
_____
_____
_____

Reflection and Discussion Questions

_____

_____

How can you as parents facilitate a personal encounter with the Person of Jesus for your children?

_____

_____

_____

_____

_____

_____

Together with Christ

Seeking our children's approval can lead to a lack of discipline in the home as they get older. We can't be afraid to clearly, consistently, and lovingly set boundaries and give guidelines. Say no when you must, yes when you can, and help them understand why you are taking a particular approach. This is part of the practice of forming our children into disciples. Teaching our children to see the good of godly authority in their parents enables them to also accept the authority of God's moral teaching. If you find discipline challenging, seek out resources that both respect the principles of Catholic teaching and apply the best of psychological science to help inform your discipline approach as parents.

Chapter 6: Husbands and Fathers

One cannot overstate the importance of the unique, irreplaceable role that fathers play in establishing, building, maintaining, and passing on the faith to their children. The spiritual vision of Christian family life is a high calling and a great adventure. It is the place where we most fundamentally live out our baptismal call as priests who lead our families in the worship of God, as prophets who pass on the faith through how we live and what we teach, and as kings who govern as servant-leaders of our families. This vision of the family and of Christian manhood is under intense spiritual attack today.

For Personal Prayer

What lies and accusations has the devil used in your life to convince you that your weaknesses and failures disqualify you before God as a husband and father?

_____
_____
_____
_____

Reflection and Discussion Questions

_____
_____
_____

Each day, ask Jesus for the full release of the spiritual power He has bestowed on you through the Holy Spirit in your baptism, confirmation, and the Sacrament of Matrimony. How can you be more be open to the working of the Holy Spirit in your life?

_____
_____
_____
_____
_____
_____

Couples' Reflection and Discussion

How can you, as a husband and father, help maintain unity and peace within your home? Does your own speech bring truth, honor, dignity, peace, and comfort to your family? What insight and affirmation can your wife provide to these questions?

_____
_____

How can you cultivate and sustain supportive friendships with other men who are rooted in Christ? How can your wife ensure that you make time for nurturing these friendships?

Together with Christ

Immaturity, particularly in men, can at times keep us from stepping confidently and selflessly into our role as parents. Spend some time in prayer before the Lord asking Him to illuminate any areas of immaturity or weakness in your attitudes and actions. It can be painful to see our failures as husbands and fathers, but only through humility can we receive the grace we need for growth. Reflect on where you need to grow most and ask your spouse to lovingly (not confrontationally or judgmentally) help encourage you to make positive changes.

Chapter 7: Wives and Mothers

As women, our identity can often be tied up in the external standards of worldly success: what we do and accomplish, how we look and what we have, who we know, and even how our kids are doing. As women of faith, we must remember the profound truth articulated by St. Teresa Benedicta of the Cross: "The world doesn't simply need what women have, it needs what women are."

For Personal Prayer

What makes it difficult for you to believe that your job as a mother is the most important job in the whole world?

_____
_____
_____
_____
_____
_____

Reflection and Discussion Questions

How have the powerful voice of shame and the lies of the devil tried to rob you of your true identity as a beloved daughter of God?

_____

_____

_____

_____

_____

_____

Couples' Reflection and Discussion

How can you cultivate and maintain strong, authentic, supportive relationships with other women whose strength is drawn from Christ's love? How can your husband ensure that you make time for nurturing these friendships?

_____

_____

_____

_____

_____

_____

Reflection and Discussion Questions

What role does Mary our Mother have in your life? How does her example of maternal care help you fulfill your vocation as wife and mother? As a husband, what Marian virtues do you see personified in your wife?

_____

_____

_____

_____

_____

_____

_____

Together with Christ

Moms can feel isolated, unappreciated, and exhausted as they try to balance the demands of home and work. It can be a struggle to remember day-to-day the immense value of your vocation as a mother. Spend some time in prayer before the Lord asking God to show you how He sees and values your offering as a wife and mother. How does it compare to how you see yourself? Share your reflections with your husband, not being afraid to be vulnerable about your own perceptions. Ask your spouse what he sees as well and if he could make a point to show his appreciation for your hidden work sometime over the next week.

Chapter 8: Building a Legacy of Love

Parents, grandparents, and mentors of young people have the important role of building a legacy of love and vibrant faith that is passed on to the next generation and beyond.

For Personal Prayer

What elders or mentors in your life have shaped your faith life? What was it about them that made their faith so attractive?

_____
_____
_____
_____
_____
_____
_____
_____

Reflection and Discussion Questions

How do you see a legacy of faith and love being lived out in your adult children and grandchildren? Or, if you do not yet have adult children or children, is there a legacy of faith being lived out in your family of origin?

_____

_____

_____

_____

_____

_____

_____

Couples' Reflection and Discussion

What are some intentional ways you can plan to or continue to help your adult children and grandchildren know Jesus?

_____

_____

_____

_____

_____

_____

_____

Reflection and Discussion Questions

Make a list of each of your children and grandchildren and commit to praying for them daily. Are there special devotions or prayers you can regularly pray as a couple for your family?

_____

_____

_____

_____

_____

_____

_____

Together with Christ

Parenting is a marathon—not a sprint! Oftentimes the physical and emotional demands of raising children can lead to exhaustion. We can be tempted to give in to discouragement or the demands of secular culture. Discuss as a couple if there have been times in your marriage—past or present—when your own discouragement distracted you from seeing the eternal worth of your efforts. What has helped to strengthen your resolve and dispel discouragement? Together write a letter to your future selves reminding one another for whom and why the tireless work of raising a family matters to you. When discouragement comes, reread your letter and ask God for His continuous help and the grace of perseverance.

Chapter 9: All Things Are Possible

Discouragement is one of the devil's most potent weapons. Our fundamental posture in this battle as parents, grandparents, and disciples is to stand on the rock that is Christ. We must keep our eyes on Him, put all our trust in His promises, and follow His leadership, and He will do the rest. Although to us humans situations can seem impossible, Jesus assures us that with God all things are possible.

For Personal Prayer

What are the small, daily ways you are giving in to annoyance and impatience with your spouse and children, and how can you nurture a more mature, self-giving love?

_____

_____

_____

_____

_____

_____

Reflection and Discussion Questions

"Be not afraid . . . open wide the doors to Christ!" Take some time to pray with these words from Pope St. John Paul the Great. Identify any fears and anxieties that keep you as a spouse or parent from living in hope and joy.

Couples' Reflection and Discussion

What elements of your family culture that are centered on the person of Jesus and the life of the Church (habits, practices, traditions, conversations) can you begin to build or reinforce?

Reflection and Discussion Questions

Take some time to share with each other what you most need prayer for right now. What do your children (and grandchildren) need prayer for? Commit either individually or as a couple to daily prayer for your spouse and the individual needs of each of your children (and grandchildren).

_____

_____

_____

_____

_____

_____

_____

Together with Christ

It can be tempting for a mom and dad to keep score of who is giving and doing more as a parent. Comparison can cause division and resentment. Family life is a team effort that requires both parents to be fully engaged—for the long haul. One way to fight comparison and resentment is to cultivate a spirit of gratitude. Practice being thankful! As a married couple or with your whole family, take time each week to thank the Lord for His goodness and provision!